OF WHEELS
AND WINGS

OF WHEELS AND WINGS

Thoughts on the Death of a Son

John Wesley White
D. Phil. [Oxford]

THOMAS NELSON PUBLISHERS
NASHVILLE

Published in Nashville, Tennessee, by Thomas Nelson, Inc., and
distributed in Canada by Lawson Falle, Ltd., Cambridge, Ontario.

Unless otherwise noted, all Scripture quotations are from the NEW
KING JAMES VERSION of the Bible, Copyright © 1979, 1980,
1982, Thomas Nelson, Inc., Publishers.

Scripture quotations noted KJV are from The Holy Bible, KING
JAMES VERSION.

Song excerpts are from "Nothing but the Blood" (Robert Lowry);
"Sweet By and By" (S. F. Bennett); "When the Roll Is Called Up
Yonder" (J. M. Black); "Tell It to Jesus" (J. E. Rankin).

Library of Congress Cataloging-in-Publishing Data

White, John Wesley.
    Of wheels and wings : thoughts on the death of a son /
    John Wesley White
       p. cm.
    ISBN 0-8407-6733-1 (pb)
    1. Bereavement—Religious aspects—Christianity. 2. White,
John Wesley. 3. White, Wes. 1954–1991. I. Title.
BV4907.W56   1992
248.8'6—dc20   92-27717
                                               CIP

1 2 3 4 5 6 7 — 97 96 95 94 93 92

To Kathleen
my Devoted Wife
and
Wes's Beloved Mother

October 4, 1991

Dearest John and Kathy:

In deepest sympathy and with my prayers:

Several weeks ago I watched a [network T.V.] documentary report on Wesley's work with the people of Canada's north. The phrase, "They trusted him," impressed me. I didn't realize at the time Wes was your son, but I know I admired the wonderful relationship he had with those dear people. You certainly gave Wesley a tremendous legacy which enabled him to be trusted by the natives, who have often seen betrayal as a way of life.

May the knowledge that in his short life he touched the lives of many with God's love, by giving them a purpose in life, give you strength and peace during your time of sorrow.

God bless and keep you.

Most sincerely,

BONNIE BOOTH
Toronto, Ontario

CONTENTS

FOREWORD

John Wesley White has been one of my Associate Evangelists for the last thirty of his nearly fifty years preaching the gospel. He began as an evangelist during school holidays, when he was barely into his teens, pitching tents in the small towns of his native Saskatchewan, Canada.

Since joining our team, he has been of invaluable personal assistance to me in the area of research. Meanwhile, he has travelled to a hundred countries around the world holding area-wide Crusades, over three hundred of which have been here in North America. In one of them, in Sioux Falls, South Dakota, well over two thousand inquirers came forward to make decisions for Christ. During his time as an evangelist, he has addressed face-to-face some six million people, two hundred thousand of whom have publicly professed Jesus Christ as Lord. In addition, for twenty years he has had a weekly, half-hour television program carried coast to coast across Canada, which is currently being seen Sunday evenings in prime-time. He is a compassionate and compellingly persuasive evangelist.

Dr. White graduated consecutively from Moody Bible Institute and Wheaton College in Illinois and in the British Isles from the Universities of Dublin and Oxford where he earned his Doctor of Philosophy degree, and

where he played hockey for the Oxford Blues. He thereafter doubled, while serving as Evangelist with me, as
Chancellor of Richmond College in Toronto for some
fourteen years.

Dr. White married Kathleen forty years ago, Wes, of
whose life and death he writes in this book, being the
second of their four sons. The White family has been a
close-knit one, as they've lived in Toronto, Canada, as
well as Ireland, England, and here in the United States.

Dr. White's purpose in writing *Of Wheels and.
Wings: Thoughts on the Death of a Son* is to glorify the
Lord, and while dealing forthrightly with how grievous
the loss of a loved one is, to point out to all those suffer-
ing bereavement who trust in Jesus Christ as Saviour and
Lord, that they need not sorrow as those who have no
hope, but look forward to that time when believers in
Christ will be forever together with our Lord.

BILLY GRAHAM
Montreat, North Carolina
January 1992

PROLOGUE

Bizarre as it may sound, I'm writing this book to myself. It's been three months since we said good-bye to Wes. Hunting for heart healing, I was told to write a letter to myself. It's run longer than I expected—into a small book. It's the first of my twenty books that I've handwritten entirely on my knees.

Job, author of arguably the oldest volume of the Old Testament, was felled "to the ground" also. He, too, had gotten word of the violent death, not of one son, but of seven, as "suddenly a great wind came from across the wilderness and struck the four corners of the house, and it fell on the young men, and they are dead. . . . Then Job fell to the ground and worshiped. And he said, 'Naked I came from my mother's womb, and naked shall I return there. The LORD gave, and the LORD has taken away; blessed be the name of the LORD' " (Job 1:19–21).

During the first trimester after Wes's death, although I've been busy traveling for Crusades and meetings—three times to Arizona, twice to Texas, once each to Oregon, California, and Pennsylvania, and tonight to Russia—these three months have been mysteriously agonizing. Kathleen, my wife, and I have fallen "to the ground" in pain and prayer. Our hearts have been ceaselessly bowed down.

But this is not a book about priceless Kathleen's grief. A mother's love is unique. Certainly, I've not known a mother who loved or sacrificed more for a son than Kathleen has for Wes. And she has wept every day, some days for hours, since, unannounced, he was taken from us. His brothers Bill, Paul, and Randy, and I'm sure his distressed widow, Sandra, have all discovered bereavement incomparably the most painful thing ever to happen to them. They could, and may, write books on this journey into a tear storm. I have no way of monitoring their inner feelings. I do know what I've felt, and as I've taken this time to write my feelings down, I can only pray that they're of help to others.

Nor are these trembling words the annals of the White family, or a recounting of my relationship to any of our other sons for whom I have exactly the same love I had—and have—for Wes. It is simply a journal of my three months of mourning. Sometimes I feel ashamed and bewildered at how poorly I have coped. Neither Kathleen nor I are good at bereavement.

However, in defense of just how culpable I have been to these disconsolate, funereal feelings, I need to point out that with reference to the newly departed, the apostle Paul did not say, "that ye sorrow not." Rather, he wrote, "That ye sorrow not, even as others which have no hope" (1 Thess. 4:13 KJV). Sometimes during the blackest hours of midnight, I've been overwhelmed that bereavement should hurt so much, only to turn to that ancient Hebrew king, the psalmist David, described as the man after God's own heart. When he received news of his son's violent death, he too wept, lamenting unashamedly, "O my son Absalom—my son, my son Absalom—if only I had died in your place! O Absalom my son, my son!" (2 Sam. 18:33).

Why publish such a painful diary? Because my experience is all too common. Since Wes's death, many grieving parents have come up to me after Crusade meetings or called or written to Kathleen and me, about their own loss of a priceless son or daughter. They say with true meaning, "We share your sorrow." On our Billy Graham Team alone, there are the Evanses, the Piatts, the Dillons, and the Fords.

In fact, it was Leighton Ford—who with his wife Jean said a reluctant and heartrending good-bye to their older son, Sandy, ten years ago last November—who encouraged me to share these feelings in a book. To all these people, and the many grieving I have not met, I bare my soul and dedicate this book.

JOHN WESLEY WHITE, D.Phil. [Oxford]
Toronto, Canada
December 29, 1991

Chapter One

*I*t had been one of those unforgettable weeks, not like black September at all. The Sunday previous to that fateful week had been my birthday, and at the morning church service Wes sat on my right and his brother Bill on my left, as their cousin, Roy, expounded to his Baptist congregation on lessons to be learned from the parable of the Prodigal Son. Wes leaned over and whispered in my ear, "Dad, that's the story you and I used to do in the Crusades."

He was alluding to the times when he and I traveled together with our Billy Graham Associate Crusade Team from New Brunswick to California and from British Columbia to Georgia. Wes flew the two of us in a leased Cessna 182 and provided multimedia pictures—three hundred to a sermon—while I preached. One of the addresses was on the Prodigal Son. For the youth sermon, Wes would load up his double carrousels with vivid cartoon drawings that depicted the runaway at home, his gallivanting down into the far-off country, the turn-around, and finally the homecoming.

All but Paul were at the birthday table that midday. He'd gone back to Baylor University in Texas where he's assistant professor of English. Wes offered the grace and what followed was all joy. The razor wit came from Bill and Randy; the hilarious humor from Wes. My role was to blow out the candles.

Wednesday noon, Kathleen and I met Wes at Shopsys across from the O'Keefe Center, Canada's number one festival hall. It is a deli in downtown Toronto, where broadcasters, newspaper columnists, lawyers with their clients, and entertainment types would lunch over a Reuben sandwich. Wes once again offered the prayer, and we discussed our trip that upcoming weekend to New York. Would he fly us down in his twin Comanche and be with us in what would doubtless be the largest evangelistic gathering to assemble in the Western world?

His eyes lit up, sparkling sky-blue like his mother's when she's excited. He would try, but he just might have to go instead to Cape Dorset in the upper Northwest Territories to buy a fresh supply of Inuit carvings for his Eskimo Art Gallery down on Queens Quay. It was acknowledged by many to be the finest of its kind in Canada. His last presentation had been to the actor Paul Newman, whose Indy car had won a world class race in July. Currently his inventory was in short supply. So he just might have to take a raincheck on the New York trip. There was, he said, the possibility that his brother Randy, also a pilot, could fly us down—provided he brought the plane home in time for him to go on up north. He said he couldn't possibly make both trips.

And then that last proposal; "Dad, some of the Inuits up there are Christians, most are not. They know you from television. How about coming up with me when you've finished those autumn Crusades? You and I'll just climb into the Comanche and go back up to Cape Dorset, and we'll have a Crusade with the Inuits. How about it?" I agreed immediately. We were both beaming when I shook Wes's hand, bonding the promise.

We topped off the deli platter with chocolate sundaes. Wes and I were both twenty pounds overweight. This habit didn't do either of us any good! But it did in precious retrospect lengthen a little our last time together. We then went out across the street. Randy's aging brown Chevrolet awaited us. But he'd forgotten to give us a door key. Wes instructed me about going to a cleaners' and getting a wire coat hanger, which I should reshape and then poke through at the top of the glass where the rubber meets the metal. He had an appointment at the bank or he'd do it for me. He embraced and kissed his mother good-bye.

Then, after he'd clamped on his helmet, mounted and started the motor, turning it around sharply, we watched him lay his big Honda motorcycle into a westward curve from Front Street into Yonge. He couldn't resist the temptation. He liked to lay even just a little rubber. It was for us his way of displaying his wheelie artistry.

His cousin Doug and he had their Hondas up to 155 miles per hour out around the Mossport racetrack the previous summer. Having such a speed freak for a son made his mother shudder, but Wes knew only too well that it gave his father a certain vicarious rush.

Wes loved wheels and wings. He had the biggest Porsche and the bluest new Pontiac made. But he liked his motorcycle and his Comanche Twin plane the best. Those wheels put his face in the wind; those wings, his eyes in the stars. At age fourteen, he bought his first motorcycle, a Norton Commando, with five hundred dollars he'd received unexpectedly from his great uncle's will. What used-motorcycle dealer would turn down a boy with that kind of cash, regardless of his age? Dad was away in a Crusade, so why not? A mother of four boys couldn't be expected to tail him everywhere. Within twenty-four hours, unbeknownst to Kathleen or me, that motorcycle had been bought, ridden by every friend in the area, piled up, and sold for parts.

Wes bought the next one after selling the family motorboat. His mother, tired of the boat's sitting in the driveway, agreed to let him sell it. He fixed it up with paint and the bribed child-labor of his youngest brother, Randy, whom he'd pay back with a few fast rides on the motorcycle he would buy. It was a brotherhood pact. With that Honda, Wes came in second in the Quebec Grand Prix. He was first, I'm now told, until the final turn when he missed the corner and crashed, but not badly enough that he didn't hoist his Honda to its wheels and, brushing the blood from his face, push it over the finish line for second place. Everybody in our neighborhood heard about it—except us, his parents. The gash in his head he just passed off as one of those things. It wasn't our first time to see him cut up.

And now we were looking at Wes riding his Honda westward with much more skill and experience. We were already looking forward to seeing him again. I got Randy's Chevy open with the coat hanger, just as Wes prescribed, and we chortled back up Yonge Street buzzing about Wes's latest one-liners and Crusade proposal. The next day Kathleen and I drove to New York, admittedly disappointed that we weren't aboard the Comanche with Wes.

That week, Harvard-trained biographer Bill Martin published his book on Billy Graham, *Prophet with Honor,* in which he stated, "Associate Evangelist John Wesley White has long been Graham's primary sermon illustrator." So I had my work cut out, as Billy had said he wanted to split his address into two parts for that Sunday afternoon, when a quarter of a million people would gather on the Great Lawn of Manhattan's Central Park. The first part would be fourteen minutes of facts about the history, sociology, and spiritual state of New York City. It was my privilege to provide the research for that part of his address.

It was also my honor to offer the invocational prayer, so I was seated on the front row between the world's two foremost gospel singers, George Beverly Shea and Sandi Patti. Behind me was Kathie Lee Gifford, who testified, and across the narrow aisle, Johnny Cash. I remember clearly that when Johnny sang I especially wished Wes had come, because Johnny had been his favorite country-western singer ever since he topped the charts with "A Boy Named Sue."

After the Crusade, Kathleen and I drove home. I had to make a quick trip to meet clergy in Marquette, Michigan, where we would be holding a Crusade the following year. It was a city where Wes and I often refueled on our travels together. Its airport and Holiday Inn were familiar places to both Wes and me. So we missed eating with Wes at Shopsys that week because, weather permitting, he planned to leave earlier than he actually did. Instead, his brother Randy flew some friends to New York. Wes delayed his departure until seven o'clock Saturday morning.

That Saturday afternoon I was at home answering television mail. Dividing my interest was a baseball game between the Blue Jays and the Twins. Suddenly, a bizarre and perhaps determinative play seized my attention. The Blue Jays were ahead, 5 to 2. As one of their chaplains, I felt they were looking good. Then Brian Harper of the Twins beat out a roller to first baseman

John Olerud, who muffed it, but recovered in time to toss the ball to John Candiotti, the pitcher who had raced over to cover first base. Harper was out, but Candiotti had stuck his right foot across first base, and Harper had unwittingly spiked him. Out came the trainer who examined the gash and then taped up Candiotti's foot. In all, it took about ten minutes. To everyone's amazement, Candiotti went back to the mound and resumed pitching. He couldn't have put out a match, let alone the Twins, after that. The boys from Minneapolis went on to win the game by a wide margin and a few days later to make mincemeat out of the Blue Jays in the American League playoffs, after which they went on to win the World Series.

Wes and Sandra owned a beautiful condominium a block from the Skydome, and living in the same building were three of the more celebrated Blue Jays. Mookie Wilson's parking space was next to Wes's. Wes would come with me when I'd address the Jays in chapel. Kelly Gruber was his casual acquaintance and his favorite baseball player. Lanny McDonald was his favorite hockey player, although he had Jerry Sawchuk's goal stick with which he blocked shots in winning the Maple Leafs' last Stanley Cup.

I remember with unforgettable vividness that inadvertent spiking of John Candiotti by Brian Harper and the taping of his foot that followed. As I'd learn twenty-two hours later, it exactly coincided with an event that would forever alter my perspective.

CHAPTER TWO

September 29, 1991. It was Sunday morning. I woke up worried, wondering how I could help our four boys more. *All parents are always thinking things like that,* I thought. That night Kathleen had dreamed about one of them going to heaven, and her Irish mother, who's been there twenty-five years, receiving him into eternal bliss. I went down and watched our half-hour television program, the first of four Canada-wide network slots every Sunday. I was preaching a pre-recorded Crusade sermon on the second coming of Christ and the comfort and hope it affords.

Then Kathleen suggested that before we left for church, we watch a television program known for its charismatic singing and preaching—an unusual request for her. Brought up Plymouth Brethren in Ireland, as Kathleen was, I was surprised—there was considerable controversy around our house about the merits of this particular television evangelist. But Kathleen's reasoning, in addition to the fact that she thought that Wes and he were look-alikes, was, "Wesley says he watches him all the time and his music and preaching bring tears to his eyes." So we watched.

Our boys' preferences go across the evangelical spectrum. Paul went to fundamentalist Briarcrest in Saskatchewan and is currently Anglican, like his two grandmothers. Wes was the most Pentecostal of our sons but Presbyterian in his subscription to Calvinism, as were his two grandfathers. (John Calvin was one Frenchman Wes liked. His brother, Paul, had written a Ph.D. thesis on the influence of John Calvin's theology.) Wes had gone to the Full Gospel Bible Institute at Eston, Saskatchewan, which is uncompromisingly Calvinist, and while he was there, our Billy Graham Associate Team held a meeting. The words of a chorus the student body sang in chapel had to do with Jesus' being alive from the dead, as the apostle Paul wrote, and consequently, "every knee should bow . . . and . . . every tongue confess that Jesus Christ is Lord" (Phil. 2:10–11). I saw tears streaming down Wes's cheeks. It was a sight I will forever cherish. I can never recall Wes's questioning basic Christian doctrine, but there were times when discipleship constraints were not his cup of tea.

For the following two years after being at the Bible Institute, he traveled with me producing the multimedia presentations for the Crusades. He liked the upbeat contemporary songs with a strong spiritual emphasis. He'd incorporate a lot of movement into his slides. He didn't care for tradition. He hated boredom. He liked me to preach strong sermons with plenty of drama. And he was ecstatic when at the gospel invitations there were bountiful harvests.

I remember the last time Wes and I were able to team up with the multimedia presentation. It was a special one-night-only Sunday evening service in a large Baptist church. The pastor, Trevor Baird, had requested the theme, "The Signs of the Second Coming of Jesus Christ," because that is what I'd preached on forty years ago in Belfast, the night his parents had come forward and made decisions for the Lord. Later, on the way home in the upper deck of a bus, Sergeant Baird asked nineteen-year-old Trevor, "If Jesus Christ were to return tonight, would you be ready?" This led Trevor and his two teenaged brothers to make decisions for Christ in that Belfast Crusade. Shortly thereafter the Bairds immigrated to this side of the Atlantic—Trevor eventually becoming pastor of this congregation, one of the largest in the country.

When I finished preaching (Wes having shown some three hundred slides to illustrate the various points) and gave the invitation, among those responding was Trevor's son Stephen, who was seventeen. Tears streaming down his cheeks, Trevor thanked Wes and me, remarking, "That makes three generations of the Bairds giving their lives to the Lord as a result of your proclaiming that theme of the coming again of Jesus Christ."

Bill, Randy, and Kathleen liked the service that Sunday morning, but I didn't. Instead of preaching, Roy showed a film about a schoolteacher who got gold stars for excellence. My mind wandered.

At noon Kathleen and I ate dinner at a restaurant called the Wildwood, a half mile from our home. I ordered Chicken Chalet, Kathleen pork ribs. We sat in the booth adjacent to the table at which we'd eaten with Wes and his brothers on my birthday. Driving home on Argonne Crescent, as we descended the hill, I remarked to Kathleen, "Here's where Wes would release Wimp and then check his speed as he raced toward our house." Wimp could hit twenty-seven miles an hour in his prime—downhill, that is!

Wimp was Wes's special dog. He described him as a huskie wrapped in a collie coat. Wes met Wimp while building up his flying hours in Arthur, Ontario. He later went on to become an airline pilot with Worldways, flying the big jets. It was there that he met and eventually married Sandra Duffy, and it was there that he met Wimp, an abandoned pup who had made himself such a nuisance to the others around the airfield that the proprietor was about to shoot him. But the love affair that has gone on from ancient times between a boy and his dog took place between Wimp and Wes. When Wes would land his rickety Beach 18 on the grass, Wimp would race like a greyhound down the runway, leap up into the quickly opened cockpit with smiling, back-slapping Wes, and together they'd taxi to the tie-down chatting it up with each other all the way. Wes fed him from rejection into true doghood with both choice meat scraps and affection. So when Wes was in the Middle East to build up flying hours, whom did I meet in our doorway when arriving home from a Crusade in Helena, Montana, but Wimp? His tail was wagging like one of the starting up props of the Beach 18, just as if he and I had been buddies from birth. I mean, he was extending to me an imploring "Welcome Home!" What could I do but reciprocate?

So with his shiny, rusty coat embellished with snow-white chest, feet, and upper nose, Wimp took canine possession of our hearth until his heartrending death a couple of years ago. A phone call was made to Wes, who carried him out into our backyard, behind the tall elm trees he and I had planted when he was a small boy. He said that he didn't want me to make the mistake of leaving Wimp's foot sticking out of the ground as I'd done when I buried our poodle Fred. We never had a dog quite like Wimp, so much like his master—modest, curious, a speed-lover, high-spirited, always wanting to please, and somehow always smiling.

So as Kathleen and I drove down Argonne, we talked affectionately about Wimp. He could turn the S curve around the corner to our house faster than most motor vehicles (unless, of course, it was Wes on his Honda or in his Porsche). But Wimp was dead, and there was that tinge of sadness whenever we'd talk about him. We just couldn't manage to drive down Argonne, ever, without remembering Wimp.

Our driveway already had three cars in it, and there was only a small space left for the little Honda Prelude that we were driving. It was where the red brick driveway butted up against the grass. Wes had left his Porsche parked there, just a few feet to the west, the whole previous winter. It was where the boat had sat too long for Kathleen and Wes had sold it for a Honda. It was where he'd park his newest Honda, remove his helmet and, if the weather was right, we'd linger and engage in small talk for the longest time. He always liked to talk about where I'd been, or where he'd been, or about the awful Leafs, or the awesome Blue Jays. Would they finally break through this October or break Torontonians' hearts again? He thought they just might win it all this time. Maybe Candiotti, with his strike-out-knuckleball, would make the difference. And Roy—Wes never thought he'd turn out to be such a good preacher. That corner of our driveway he'd ridden, driven, or walked through perhaps ten thousand times. And it was the spot from which as a teenager he perfected his hockey slapshot, which terrorized goalies from Toronto to Boston to Chicago to St. Petersburg, Florida.

So that spot on the driveway was where we pulled in. To our right we noticed Kathleen's three sisters driving by, then backing up Argonne. The taillights seemed to be flashing blood-red. Mary got out of the driver's seat and Ruth from the passenger side. None of them smiled. Their heads were bowed down as if it were pouring rain. Mary came to Kathleen and Ruth to me. Mary asked Kathleen to come into the house. That was odd.

Ruth, known to the family as the truth-teller, is the youngest of Kathleen's five Irish sisters. Petite and pretty, this time she looked pale and frightened, and her voice rocketed up in pitch as she blurted, "I've got terrible news!" Despite the anguish on her face, I was totally unprepared for what was to come. "Wes was killed yesterday in his plane in Quebec!"

My head went into a dizzy whirl. I felt I couldn't breathe. It was like the world had come to an end. As Ruth burst into tears, I heard Kathleen shriek to her soft-spoken sister, Mary, "Where is he? What hospital is he in?"

I gazed at the faded pink unilock bricks in the driveway. They flamed as if coming red-hot out of the kiln, rising like cannon balls to strike me. The noonday sun seemed to descend like a falling star, with palpable darkness wrapping me in a shroud. My knees went rubbery, my heart leapt into my mouth, the Chicken Chalet in my stomach churned, and I wanted to vomit. My head went into a spin as though bolted to a paint-shop mixer. Was I slipping over the edge to insanity? Shafts of pain coursed through me. For a moment I thought the hammering of my heart was a massive, fatal heart attack. *If so, I want to go quickly; how about right now? If Wes is gone, I want to go too.*

I rushed into the house. Kathleen was still demanding hysterically, "Where is he? What hospital is he in?" I threw my arms around her and said, "Wesley is with the Lord! The Lord hath given; the Lord hath taken away.

Blessed be the name of the Lord!" Kathleen kept exclaiming, "My son, Wesley! My son, Wesley!"—words she has exclaimed thousands of times since, sometimes in loud lamentation, sometimes in soft whispers, as she awakens out of sleep at three or four o'clock in the morning.

When I surrendered Kathleen to her three tender-loving sisters, our oldest son, Bill, threw his arms around me, as I had him and our other sons when they were small boys in Oxford. And he said again and again, "Dad, he's in heaven ahead of you, like you've always talked about, and you'll see him again and forever. And Wes—he's done more living than nearly anybody else does in seventy or eighty years!"

Bill performed like a tiger that week of deepest grief. Heartbroken as all of us were, he kept his head up and held us steady. He has a remarkably high I.Q. tempered with rock-solid stability. He was the take-charge member of the family that week.

I hardly remember how many minutes it was before Kathleen and I were able to regain a modicum of composure, sufficient to hear what had happened. Wes had taken off from the Island Airport at the Toronto harbor front Saturday morning en route to the upper Arctic. He had refueled at Rouyn, Quebec. Then he had flown the long leg into LeGrande in northern Quebec. At two o'clock the weather was fine, but higher up there was a front moving in. So he waited until 3:30, and on takeoff his right motor had sputtered. The plane lurched sharp right, at forty or fifty feet off the runway, and the wing went down. No pilot on earth could have controlled it at that height. The wing caught in the ground, the nose followed, and the whole plane broke up like a crushed peanut shell. Wes had no chance. He was killed instantly.

Bill had just gotten confirmation from the French po-
liceman up at LeGrande, Quebec, who had witnessed the
crash. Wes's wife, Sandra, had been notified. Bill had
also called the morgue in Montreal. It was Wes all right.
There was no hope that it was all a terrible mistake. Like
Job, what I feared most had really happened. Terror had
struck at noon.

Wes had gone to his eternal home. The finality of it
made us feel we were under an avalanche, from which we
wondered if we could ever be dug out. Kathleen was
wedged lovingly between her sisters, whose tears poured
down their cheeks and mingled with hers. I disappeared
down to the basement and out the back. It was where Wes
buried Wimp. It was where Wes and the boys—but mostly
Wes and I—had put up a cedar fence to hedge in a hockey
rink in the winter. And come spring, we'd play soccer and
balloon ball out there. One summer it was a go-cart racetrack. The whole neighborhood of boys streamed in, and we
even had it suggested to us that we sell tickets as if it were
a miniature Mossport or Indianapolis.

I paced for most of the next hour round and round
that quadrangle, asking, "Lord, why? Why not me? My
mother went! Dad went! That's in the expected order.
That seemed heartrending enough. But this, Lord, seems
insane. God, why did it happen?

"I know, Lord, what I said to Kathleen, 'the Lord
hath given and the Lord hath taken away. . . .' But,
Lord, if you'll pardon me at this moment, I just don't
have it in me to say, 'Blessed be the name of the Lord!'
I know, Lord, I will after a little time has passed and it's
all explained, but just now I can't. Is that okay?"

There seemed to be no answer. Heaven was silent.

CHAPTER THREE

Most professional people, over the long haul, cultivate a heavy coverall for their feelings. I'm no exception. Slipping quietly back into the walk-out basement door of our home, I was seething with anger, disbelief, grief, and a wound that left me wishing I, let alone Wes, had never been born. A plethora of unanswered questions raced through my head. Why is there birth if there has to be death? Why didn't I take a course or at least read a book on how to cope with the unexpected death of a son? Wes had twelve thousand hours of flying experience, having taken off and landed the biggest commercial airline jets in the busiest airports in the world, and having flown earlier as a bush pilot from the riskiest of runways and in the worst weather, five years through the Arctic. Why would Wes have crashed on a beautiful Saturday afternoon?

Did they put jet fuel into his tank by mistake, or maybe even some water? Why did it take twenty-one hours for them to notify Sandra when his flight plan had on it both their home and business phone numbers? Was it sludge or sediment, or some alien liquid they carelessly dumped into his motor? Was it because a cover-up was taking place? My anger superceded my anguish at that moment. And finally, as his father, why was I not up there, lying out on that airfield to buffer the death-blow to his body? The flames of indignation and misapprehension were roaring.

19

But I needed to go back in the house. Precious Kathleen and dear Bill and forlorn Randy needed me, and there was that heartrending phone call to be made to Paul in Texas. Neighbors and relatives were pouring into the house, saying, "He was the nicest guy!"

"He never had an enemy."

"I'll never get over it."

"He was so exciting to be around!"

"He's done it all, and there was nothing more on earth for Wes to do!"

"Why is it that the good guys go and the bad ones stay?"

"He was always the life of the party."

Yes, and others were saying, "To live is Christ and to die is gain."

"Blessed are the dead, who die in the Lord!"

"And don't forget that Jesus said, 'This day shalt thou be with Me in paradise!' So he's far better off than he would be here!"

All those appropriate remarks were so beautifully said, with heartfelt tears and trembling handshakes, but the words seemed empty. They ran off my heart like water off a duck. Probably the worst case was the woman who offered with perfect sincerity, "I know exactly how you feel. Two years ago my grandmother in England died from cancer at the age of eighty-seven, and I know exactly how you feel!"

It seemed the best words were no words, just a warm handshake, an embrace with a prompt release, or a sympathetic look with a genuine falling tear. Just to be there, that was enough. Everyone meant well. But at a time like that everything that's said seems to have a raw edge.

It took an hour—felt like a year—to get through to Paul. He had been to church and then out to Sunday dinner and was a time-zone behind. All the time I wondered, *Shall I tell him Wes had an accident, and he should stand by for further word? Or should I just blurt it out: "Wes has been killed"?*

In age, like Bill and Wes, Wes and Paul were only fifty-five weeks apart. Sons of an itinerant evangelist since they were born, they strutted their stuff and claimed proudly that they'd been to nineteen schools and that's why they knew so much more than Dad, who'd taken his first ten grades in a one-room rural schoolhouse out in Saskatchewan. When they were four, five, and six, in Oxford, England, Paul, Wes, and Bill started singing three-part harmony; and two years later, up in Scotland, they were given three gleaming silver trumpets. It was, to their doting parents, a veritable miracle how in no time they could harmonize and even triple-tongue. The competition to achieve and excel was always a factor for the three eldest boys. Their fashion-conscious mother had them looking like they had just stepped out of a band box up on stage. They looked and sounded like angels. Bill and Randy had the pretty faces of their mother, Paul was the in-betweener, and Wes—well, maybe it was because he got nailed with his name—he was, everybody said, like his dad.

One night in England, we learned later, they drew two of the Beatles into the Central Hall in Liverpool to hear them. The Beatles likened them to a miniature edition of "The Monkees." Drawing crowds for their father's preaching, the boys sang and played their way around Britain in personal appearances, on BBC-TV and ITV. And all the way to the meetings we would talk.

Their rapid-fire questions were sometimes so incisive or way-out that there were occasions I felt I didn't have the brains to have a headache. The boys would sleep on the way home on a bed in the back of our station wagon. Claiming turf became a refined science during those night rides.

They were as close as peas in a pod, and if anyone else took on a White, he took on all four. Our boys could fight and argue because all their blood was Irish. Their mother's first cousin, Rinty Monaghan, was the world flyweight boxing champion, so they learned early now and then to punch each other out. If ever brothers were brothers, it was those four.

So trying to get through to Paul was doubly agonizing. New arrivals at the house included a young Jewish doctor who kindly broke into his holiday at Bill's behest to prescribe sedatives for Kathleen and me. Kathleen agreed immediately. I waved them off, wouldn't hear of taking a pill. The "Gos-Pill" was what I'd preached since I was fifteen, and I didn't need any other pills, even now. How wrong I was! Three nights in nearly three months I tried to sleep without them, each time not getting a wink. Those reenactments mentally of the crash— they just wouldn't go away.

Finally, Paul answered. *Could I tell him?* Wes was not just his big brother. They were best friends. For years, Paul—who played for the junior Nationals (the same season as did Wayne Gretzky), and later won the scoring championship for the All-England Hockey League while working on his Ph.D. and playing for the Bristol Rovers—would stickhandle the puck away from hockey fiends checkmating him, so they thought, only to have him thread, fire, flick, or feather a pass through to his big right-wing brother, and Wes would bury it. Wristshots, slapshots, backhanders, deflections, flips, one-timers—Wes had mastered them all, and strong and determined as he was, few defensemen could body-check him out of the slot. He wasn't averse to kicking the odd one in. And Wes would get Paul free flying passes. Paul once got Wes a job as a pilot in Texas, only they couldn't wangle a green card.

"Hey, Dad!" Paul sounded upbeat. "The Blue Jays really blew it yesterday!"

All I could think to ask was, "Paul, was the preacher good this morning?"

"Yeah, he was all right. How's Mom and Bill and Randy?" I paused, but he kept going. "Did Wes fly up to the Arctic?"

"Yes, Paul, he got most of the way up, but I've got terrible news. Wes was killed yesterday afternoon!" Silence. Choking. I hadn't heard him cry like that since he fell off his beat-up bike in Rexdale. It's heartbreaking to hear a son, a mature professor of English, crying as he did. The moments it took for him to compose himself were like eternity for me. Like me, he was stabbed in the heart; he was grief-stricken, disbelieving. Finally he said, "Let me talk to Mom!" Then it was to Bill and Randy. They did little else than sob and reaffirm their love. "Could it actually be true?" "Yes, it was true."

Within minutes, he had set up his plane connections and telephoned that he was on the way. By nine o'clock that night he was walking through arrivals looking pale and forlorn, as he flung himself into his brokenhearted mother's arms. The other four of us had left a house full of relatives and friends to go and meet Paul. It all seemed so unbelievable. Bill and Randy tried to smile,

but I saw more tears than teeth. As the five of us hud-
dled, I tried to pray. But the words were miserably slow
and few, and short of an amen, I just gave up.

Meanwhile, there were other calls to make, one to
Wes's Uncle Lewis, the Saskatchewan farmer of whom
he was so fond. He would get into Regina and be down
tomorrow, even though it was harvest time. Kathleen
called her relatives spread from Belfast to Lethbridge.
They had to be made mostly on Bill's second phone,
because the calls coming in were so many. Virtually our
whole Billy Graham Team called. Billy and Ruth tried to
call us from Switzerland, but the phone was continually
busy.

Billy's pastor, Calvin Thielman, summed them all
up. He had stayed with us in Oxford. He has three boys.
Calvin cried during most of the conversation, and he said
he knew everybody would be trying to say, " 'We know
what you're going through,' but nobody knows like God
the Father. He gave His only begotten Son, so He
knows."

When I preached the following Sunday evening in
that twelve-thousand-seat arena in Tucson, Arizona, because of what Calvin said, for the first time in memory
my text was John 3:16, "For God so loved the world that
He gave His only begotten Son, that whoever believes in
Him should not perish but have everlasting life." That
was what Billy Graham preached to a quarter-of-a-mil-
lion gathered the previous Sunday in New York, but
only now was I beginning to realize what the Father
gave when He sent His Son to be the Savior of the
world. One of the illustrations I gave to Billy for that
sermon (he didn't use it) was the newspaper account that
weekend of how the accidental death of Eric Clapton's

son had so shattered Clapton that he was completely immobilized. All he could do was sing his composition dedicated to his late son, "Tears in Heaven." Little did I know that before that week had run its course, Wes would be killed, and I'd be similarly distraught.

Bill, Paul, and Randy stood ten feet tall during those Gethsemane days between Sunday, the darkest midnight we had ever experienced, and the funeral that took place on Thursday.

Bill and I went to Sandra's parents' house, where a blanket of gloom had settled. Sandra was devastated. We prayed together and went through the painful process of trying to arrange the funeral. It would be held in People's Church with Dr. Paul Smith presiding. He had baptized the boys when Wes was a teenager. Billy Graham's older son, Dr. William Franklin Graham, Jr., would preach the funeral sermon.

Franklin and Wes had gone together to LeTourneau College, a Christian liberal arts school in Longview, Texas, and that's where they both had begun flying. Wes had just turned seventeen. We took him along with his brothers, Paul and Randy, en route to the Black Congress on Evangelism held in Houston, during the first days of 1972. I was standing in for Billy Graham. E. V. Hill presided. The singing and preaching there were, in spirit, beyond anything our boys had ever heard or beheld. They were awestruck. Could heaven be this good?

Four months later, Kathleen and I were back at LeTourneau with Randy and with our two snow-white poodles, Tanya and Fred. Upon arrival, we inquired, "Where is Wes?" He was out at the airfield where a marvelous, strong woman ran the flying school. When Wes dropped out of the sky onto the runway and taxied up, he jumped out smiling and gestured for his mother, Randy, and me to get into the plane. Kathleen hesitated, so that marvelous woman said she'd go too. Kathleen and Randy sat in the back seat, each holding a poodle. I'd have to stay on the ground. I watched them take off. They seemed to be gone a long time. They flew over to Arkansas, and coming back, Wes exhorted his mother and Randy to hang on. The marvelous woman turned around and reassured them, tongue-in-cheek, that this was all a part of Wes's training. He went into stalls, nosedives, barrel rolls, and I really don't know what! I just know that Kathleen has never been in a small plane since. Tanya quietly died a few weeks later. And Randy was hooked. He would become a pilot, just like his big brother!

Franklin has been a close friend of our family for at least a dozen years. I've served on his Samaritan Purse/World Medical Mission Boards for both Canada and the United States, and he preaches two or three nights in most of the Crusades that it's my privilege to conduct. Those sermons are carried across Canada on my television program. So when we called, he said he'd come any time, day or night, and even if he had another engagement, he would cancel it and come.

And with Franklin would come, all the way from San Diego at his own expense, Dennis Agajanian, who, according to Johnny Cash, is "the world's fastest flat pickin' guitarist." He'd sing Wes's favorite song, "Nothing but the Blood": "What can wash away my sin? Nothing but the blood of Jesus. What can make me whole again? Nothing but the blood of Jesus. Oh, precious is the flow, that washes white as snow, no other fount I know, nothing but the blood of Jesus!" In all our Crusades since Wes's funeral, Dennis has sung that song and dedicated it to Wes's memory. And if it moves the crowds as much as it moves me, then I feel the Lord may have Dennis sing that one before the hosts of heaven in eternity. Maybe I'll request it!

ðə ðə ðə

It was thirty years ago, as 1962 was about to be ushered in in Glasgow, Scotland. Scots call it Hogmanay. Every loony north of the Tweed was out celebrating that night, many with whiskey bottles in their hands. Over two thousand Scots were shoehorned into the Tent Hall, a legacy of Dwight L. Moody. Bill, Wes, and Paul were singing and blowing their trumpets. Wes was next to me and, though a year younger than Bill, was by a tad the tallest of the three. They finished the chorus, "Nothing but the blood of Jesus" and up went their trumpets gleaming in the spotlights, Wes's the highest by an inch or two. His cheeks were ballooned out and his eyes were aglow, sky-blue like his mother's. And there was an angelic, celestial *shekinah* on his face—the kind that I think I read about in the Revelation of Jesus Christ—which is on his countenance right now.

CHAPTER FOUR

Funerals are always difficult, but making the arrangements for Wes's was especially so, because various members of the two families had to keep excusing themselves to run into washrooms and cry. Kane's of North York is a palatial funeral home, but it doesn't have enough washrooms.

My own parents' funerals were sad events for me, but it's to be expected that parents die a generation, say, before their children. But to have said good-bye to a son who carries your whole name, your genes, and a lion's share of your hopes for tomorrow—that, to a mortal like me, is pain well beyond my emotional reach. But, like it or not, we faced up to television and newspaper reporters, which involved fumbling around for a photo of Wes that would do him proud. Drafting the obituary was really hard, incorporating all the adjectives that various relatives wanted in, any words seeming inadequate at a time like that. And there were—in addition to the back-to-back phone calls which came from as far away as Australia—telegrams, cards, candy boxes, flowers, and plants.

Our house still has eighteen of those plants, and every time I come home I feel an obsessive obligation to water them and turn them, where I can, to the sunlight which has, until this week, been diminishing with each passing day. The flowers are now fading, but they're still around. I'm trying to appreciate flowers again, to smell the roses. They're still too much a death reminder. Some of the faded pink petals are like little knives in the heart.

We had tried initially to arrange the funeral for Tuesday. But various obstacles delayed us: the twenty-one hour delay in notifying Sandra, red tape in the Montreal morgue, the language barrier which rightly or wrongly no one believed existed, and the bureaucracy between the morgue and two funeral homes. We had a terrible lingering question about whether there would or would not be an open casket. It had us all in a black hole. John Kane, the funeral director, decided the coffin would be kept closed, explaining sensitively that Wes's body was terribly broken up.

Younger than Wes, John throughout was so very kind and helpful. Kathleen, standing beside the coffin, immediately after the funeral, blinded by her tears, once mistook him for a well-known nephew, threw her arms around him in a protracted embrace, and flooded his tuxedo with tears. Since Kathleen is so beautiful, I suspect John has forgiven her for a case of mistaken identity.

At first, the Wednesday afternoon visitation was to have been held in a usual facility. But the crowd promised to be so large that John decided to hold the initial visitation in the funeral home's usual facility in the afternoon, and then move the evening visitation to its largest chapel.

In addition to the stories in *The Toronto Star, The Sun,* and *The Globe and Mail,* Jerry Howarth had announced Wes's death to the whole Blue Jay baseball network across Canada. Peter Durrant, the CTV reporter who had on Wes's previous trip gone with him to the Arctic and produced a brilliant news story on his work among the Inuits (he said they call Wes "Santa Claus"), did a second story on Wes's death. On the Monday evening news, he said that there was an Inuit who professed to be a carver, who'd gotten drunk and committed a minor crime, for which he was imprisoned until he could pay a twenty-five hundred dollar fine. He heard that "Santa Claus" had come to town and asked if he would come over and see him. Wes wasn't sure whether or not he knew him, but he dipped into his pocket, paid the fine in cash, told the guy to carve him a stone bear, and said he'd see him the next time he came up. Wes was on his way up on September 28, but at 3:30 P.M. he went up instead to the land above the stars.

Our family spent special time with Wes's body before the public was let in. It seemed so unnatural, senseless, and grim that his body was locked up in that shiny, dark brown box with the gleaming metallic appointments. It was a paradox that the fragrance of flowers filled one's nostrils with a sense of degenerating mortality: it was more like a stench than a sweet aroma. At that moment, I felt enclosed in a sarcophagus of gloom. It was one occasion in my life when I tried to open my mouth wide in the hope of the Lord filling it with some words of consolation to a totally devastated family. None came.

The Sunday night after getting the news of Wes's death, I had prowled the streets from midnight to dawn, retracing what I thought might have been the pavement marks Wes and his friends made twenty years ago, when they had cruised and laid rubber on the neighborhood tarmac. They seemed now to be angelic footprints that I could nearly feel with my feet.

The night before the funeral, around midnight, we'd driven around that palatial-appearing funeral home. I'd gotten out and looked in every window. A police car sat vigilant nearby, but the officer made no move. He had apparently seen sights like that before. But walking around that funeral home in the anonymity of midnight! *Where was Wes?* It was as if I was standing outside Buckingham Palace with the gates and doors all firmly closed. I felt, for the first time, so cut off from my son. I yearned for the funeral director to open a side door and take me to wherever Wes was in that place. Then, *why couldn't I see Wes raised from the dead, as the apostle Paul saw his nephew Eutychus brought back to life?* It was a flash hope. Then the helplessness and gloom descended again like yellow rain.

And now, bowed to our lowest posture ever, as Kathleen, Bill, Paul, Randy, and I stood around that sealed box, indescribable images flashed through our minds. Where nature could find all the tears that flowed, I don't know. Paul blurted out in exasperated desperation, "I just want to see his face." There would be no more looking at Wes's "I-getcha," laughing face on this earth. There was a terrifying moment when I feared that Paul might even break into the casket. Perhaps mercifully, John Kane walked in at that point to intimate that our time was up. But if weeping comes in waves, that was the highest wave that day! We all felt that we were so low down we had to look up to see bottom. We really did.

There was a brief break for a little sustaining tea as John Kane had the coffin moved down into the large chapel. There, the crowds streamed in. There were Pastor Paul and Anita Smith, with whom we had the closest possible family ties for most of our boys' lives. Anita and Kathleen were natives of Ulster, and having laughed together as only the Irish can, they now cried together.

And there was David Mainse, who prayed in a corner courageously with us Whites, who were so emotionally paralyzed that we could scarcely pray for ourselves. Ken Campbell, Canada's highest profile anti-abortionist, was so affirming! And Wes's cousin Brian—perhaps as a doctor he knew better than most when to speak and when not to speak—just stood in front of us and looked for the longest time before saying anything. It certainly seemed to me to be the right thing for him to do.

Dennis Agajanian and Franklin Graham came in and spent most of their time with Kathleen. "Why, Franklin, do you—and why did Wes—have this seemingly irrepressible urge to fly?" she asked.

"Because," replied Franklin with the utmost of empathy, "it's in your blood. You're like a human bird. When you take off and ascend into the sky, that's where you really feel free! A real pilot is someone who just has to fly."

Every time since, when Kathleen has seen Franklin, she asks him the same question. And he gives her the same answer. It's a cyclic conversation that will perhaps go on for years to come. And it's as regular as clockwork. But it's therapeutic. Each time she and Franklin have that verbal exchange, she tells each of her sisters on the telephone.

David Mainse had announced Wes's funeral arrangements across the continent on his "100 Huntley Street" program. Wes had great affection for and fascination with David Mainse, whose handsome profile he always thought resembled "The Six Million Dollar Man." Their last meeting was in Copp's Coliseum in Hamilton at a Billy Graham Crusade. Kathleen, Wes, and a friend of Wes's sat behind David Mainse on the platform.

The biblical David wrote that the Lord inhabits the praises of His people, and among David Mainse's greatnesses is the fact that he constantly praises the Lord. Kathleen and I reintroduced him to Wes and his friend. Wes many times retold the encounter with the dramatic inflections he engaged in his storytelling (he was a fan of Rich Little, who grew up here in Ontario). David had asked, "Wes, are you married?" Wes having replied in the affirmative, David remarked, "Well, praise God for married men!" He then asked, "And what do you do for a living?" Receiving Wes's reply, he responded, "Well, praise God for airline pilots." He then turned to Wes's friend and inquired, "And what do you do?" Receiving his reply, David responded, "Well, praise God for cement-truck drivers!" He then asked, "And are you married?" Receiving the word that he was not, David observed, "Well, praise God for single men!"

It is my belief that currently Wes is up there around the throne of Jesus Christ, praising the Lord as David Mainse is doing so correctly here on earth. And he may even have a crescent of newly arrived saints around him telling stories about when he was down there on earth, and very likely, about this one when he last met David Mainse.

CHAPTER FIVE

October 3 was crisp but sunny. Since Wes's death the previous Saturday, there had been a hard frost, and the flowers that fringed our front lawn were fading fast. Out in the back, trees Wes and I had planted twenty-five years ago were turning autumnal colors. Summertime had passed. Fall had arrived and Canadian winter would not be far behind.

Visitors from near and far streamed into our house. Dr. John Corts, the Executive Vice-President and Chief Operating Officer of the Billy Graham Evangelistic Association, was one. John's comforting words from the Old Testament book of Job, chapters 1 and 42, have had much meaning for me. Job had seven sons and three daughters. Then came the holocaust that wiped them all away. Later, when God restored Job, He gave him "twice as much as he had before" (42:10). But then why do the Scriptures mention his then fathering only seven sons and three daughters? That doesn't sound like twice as many. John explained that whereas Job lost forever the stock and possessions he'd had earlier, he hadn't really lost his previous sons and daughters. They were as much alive—indeed more so—than his seven sons and three daughters on earth. So Job did indeed have "twice as many" children as before. It's so comforting to Kathleen and me to know that we still have four living sons, not three.

John and I talked about the many Crusades he set up for us when Wes and his brothers were singing and playing their trumpets. There was Twin Falls, Idaho, where Evel Knievel, a one-time hero of Wes's, lived—and whose wife came forward in one of our meetings. There were Billings, Montana; Decatur, Illinois; and Waterloo, Iowa.

And there was the Crusade in Gibson City, Illinois, in 1966 where the boys learned to play baseball. George Beverly Shea still reminds us of the last night there. The boys, by this time including Randy, sang and played the song he composed aboard the Queen Mary while crossing the Atlantic to Billy's historic Harringay Crusade: "Oh the wonder of it all . . . that God loves me!" Only they sang it, "Oh the wonder of it all . . . that Jesus loves me!" because they needed an extra syllable to keep their three-part harmony in rhythm. Bev called me recently to say it was that night that the famous newscaster, Bob Williams, as a teenager, was converted. Bev said Billy Graham gave Bob his only interview at the time of the outbreak of Desert Storm, the occasion of Billy's being in the White House with the Bushes. I told Wes about it only months before his death. His face lit up like a Christmas tree.

And who else came around to the house? Well, there was Dr. Robert Thompson arriving with Franklin Graham. He had come from British Columbia just to be with us in our hour of grief. At the time of the last coalition government in Ottawa, Dr. Thompson was perhaps the most powerful politician in Canada. We chatted a little about politics. How was his friend, Prime Minister Brian Mulroney, doing? Better, he thought, than he was showing in the polls. I told him, because we were talking about Wes, that the Honorable Len Gustafson (who had nominated Mr. Mulroney for the leadership of the Conservative Party and was currently Parliamentary Secretary to the Prime Minister) was the Member of Parliament for the constituency where I was brought up, where my brother Lewis lives on our Saskatchewan farm, and where Wes had spent so much time. It was Len who called and asked if I would come and speak with Mr. Mulroney about some of the issues that are eating at the unity of the country. Wes flew the Toronto-Ottawa route for City Express Airways at the time, so I flew up on one of the Dash 8s of which he was captain.

Wes caught me, I told Bob, in one of his many jokes. He enjoyed doing that. Mr. Mulroney may be a handsome man, but he has a jaw that makes him a cartoonist's dream. So Wes had turned to me and said, "Dad, you're from Saskatchewan. There's a city out there which is named for the Prime Minister." I replied with fatherly condescension, "That's not possible, Wes, because all the Saskatchewan cities were named before Mr. Mulroney was ever born." Wes came back with the smile and twinkle which were a trademark of his humor, "Dad, you're wrong! The city named for the Prime Minister is Moose Jaw!" Bob Thompson smiled wryly, but he didn't laugh. Nor did I. It was not a day for laughter.

When Kathleen and I got to The People's Church, traditionally known as Canada's largest Protestant congregation, we were led into an ample private room, where I could see the people arriving, but Kathleen couldn't. Among those who came from near and far were many leading members of our Billy Graham Team I didn't expect. With Dr. John Corts were Dr. Sterling Huston, Tom Bledsoe, John Dillon, Grover Maughon, Sherman Barnette, Hank Beukema, and Dan Southern.

Dan had set up the New York rally of 250,000 and had, with his wife, Lori, entertained Wes and Sandra in his home in Minneapolis. Son of a physician and a college wrestler standing at 6'6", Dan stepped in when one of Wes's pallbearers was so grief-stricken that he ran off to do his grieving in solitude.

Sterling Huston has directed all of Billy Graham's great North American Crusades for twenty years. Prior to that, he set up several of those in which it was my privilege to be the evangelist and for which the boys played and sang. He was a prominent Youth for Christ director when in 1966 the boys sang and played their trumpets and I preached the last series of meetings held by Youth for Christ International in the famous Billy Sunday tabernacle at Winona Lake in Indiana. Billy Graham preached the finale. Tens of thousands of evangelical Christians, and especially leaders, will be forever grateful for spiritual experiences they had while Youth for Christ International held its great annual conferences there for two decades.

And John Dillon! Wes loved John, whose two first names were also John Wesley. John had been director of our Billy Graham Associate Crusades for many years. When Wes was going through his toughest times as a teenager, John would do things like taking him to see the Detroit Tigers and telling him little jokes that he never forgot. Wes reminded John of his middle son, Chuck, a baseball whiz who died of leukemia at the age of twenty in the same hospital and almost simultaneous to Dwight D. Eisenhower. Chuck had given his life to Christ several years earlier in a Leighton Ford Crusade in Aberdeen, South Dakota. I would use Chuck's story as an illustration and Wes would listen closely.

Of the many Crusade coordinators who knew Wes, Lew Blanchard knew him the best. They would go fishing together, and it was to Lew that Wes said, "You know, I think the Lord has called me to preach. Dad sure thinks so. Someday I may get around to it. It may take time." Time has now given way to eternity, but Wes's dad thinks Wes did a lot of great service for the Lord, even though he never became a preacher.

The moment arrived that Kathleen and I had been dreading most, walking down the aisle for the funeral of our priceless son. That aisle, I'm sure, was for Kathleen just as long as it was for me. I looked at it through blinding tears and thought I would sooner have walked barefoot to Buenos Aires. As we entered under the sweep-around gallery, there was the coffin staring at us. It was as if the grim reaper stood over it with gloating eyes, saying, "I've gotcha this time." I braced myself, as I embraced Kathleen. Could we make it without turning into a couple of weeping, distraught parents who were acting as if our beliefs had failed us? Hadn't I heard and read of great Christians and saintly missionaries who had stared death in the eye and defied it? Where was my faith?

The first couple of steps were okay. I have no idea what happened to Kathleen. I think she was exceedingly brave. Then I lost it completely. The harder I tried not to, the more I cried out loud. That coffin! It looked like Mount Everest! It was as if for a moment there was a flicker of candlelight at the end of the tunnel, and suddenly a big bad hand snuffed it out. The Sahara in July; Siberia in January; I would gladly walk across either or both, I thought, if I could escape this. That front pew seemed light years away.

Apparently we made it. Bill, Paul, and Randy reportedly closed in around us and Pastor Paul Smith got the church singing. By our request it was one of the songs the boys sang on their "Trumpets of the Lord" album, since Wes was at this moment already "there." "There's a land that is fairer than day; and by faith we can see it afar. For the Father waits over the way; to prepare us a dwelling place there. In the sweet by and by; we shall meet on that beautiful shore. In the sweet by and by; we shall meet on that beautiful shore."

That settled Kathleen and me down a little. But it took the last verse to settle us in for what followed: "To our bountiful Father above; we will offer our tribute of praise; for the glorious gift of His love; and the blessings that hallow our days."

Wes's Uncle Elmer, husband of my sister, Betty, led in prayer. At the family get-togethers he always led the prayers, whether it was Christmas, New Year's, or a wedding. He has a special gift in public intercession, to lift everybody—who wants by faith to be lifted—to the regions of the Throne of Grace.

Then Wes's Uncle Billy, a clergyman and Kathleen's only brother, made remarks about the night Wes was born. It was in his grandfather and grandmother Calderwood's house in Belfast. Wes's grandparents, said Billy, were in heaven and, as Kathleen dreamed before we got the news, Wes had joined them the previous Saturday. It caused me to envisage his entrance into the Lord's eternal presence.

Wes was an expert at grand entrances on earth, let alone this, his grand entrance into heaven. There seemed to be no place on earth where Wes wasn't welcome. He just had that indescribable gift of setting people at ease.

There would be an immediate camaraderie that said, "I'm here, how are you?" He had that infectious look that made people feel good about themselves. He would never knock on our door; he'd just arrive! I would jump up and put on the kettle for tea while his mother kissed him, and then it was straight to the kitchen. It was as if he was born for arrivals—whether in a church, at a party, in the principal's office, or a hockey penalty box. (Wes spent more time in penalty boxes during hockey games than his other three brothers combined.) Peter Durrant, the CTV broadcaster, said that when he and Wes arrived in his Comanche up in Cape Dorset he would circle two or three times. The whole village would turn out. Then he would land, and they would raise a "Whoopee, Wes's here!" He was so completely uninhibited, so totally disarming.

Wes really had that thing called charisma that no one can define. It was a delicate balance of contagious modesty and an unacknowledged love for the wide stage and the one-man act. Everywhere he went, effortlessly it seemed, he emerged as the life of the party. He always generated excitement and would spread it around like a circus clown radiates laughter. He was a natural, jovial pied piper at the front of a parade out for a lark. Bill, Paul, and Randy went to a "night after the funeral" held by Peter Durrant, where a hundred of Wes's friends celebrated North York's "beloved prankster" of twenty years ago. They showed slides and movies of him doing everything imaginable, matched by ovations that apparently resembled those of a sporting event. At the end, Peter left Wes's life-size picture on the screen long enough for everybody there to spontaneously go up and kiss him good-bye. The guy with the most macho reputation of all, I'm told, went up three times.

So his Uncle Billy told about his being born in the Calderwood home in Belfast. As he did so, I recalled vividly that he had arrived a little earlier than expected. I was preaching during the precise hour of his birth on December 5, 1954, to three thousand people in Glasgow, Scotland, in the Odeon Theater. One of those born again the same hour Wes was being born was the distinguished nutritional scientist, Dr. Douglas McDougal. I heard him many years later on the BBC-TV national news, which is carried evenings throughout the British Isles.

When Dennis had sung, "Nothing but the Blood of Jesus," Franklin read the 23rd Psalm, expounding the gospel of Christ as clearly and simply as his father ever did. Franklin's emphasis on "Yea, though I walk through the valley of the shadow of death, I will fear no evil: for thou art with me" had a special calming and comforting effect on those of us who were most disconsolate. He concluded by telling those in the congregation how to be saved, so that at all times they may be ready for death.

I will remember forever the evening Wes said to me over twenty years ago, "Dad, I want to be saved! Would you kneel down with me and pray that prayer with me that you do in the Crusades, so that I can be sure I'm saved?" In retrospect, those minutes that followed just might be the most meaningful investment of my time I have ever made as an evangelist. It was in his upstairs room in the northeast corner of our North York home. That spot where we knelt together beside his bed is a hallowed one for me. There's never been a spaceship launched from Cape Canaveral that has soared even a fraction of the distance I soared that evening. Two days after Wes's death one of his Bible school teachers, Owen Scott, sent words of great meaning to Kathleen and me through the Reverend Lorne Pritchard: "I am sure he was saved . . . [Wes] was so tender." Sensitive as parents are at a time such as that, Kathleen and I found those words precious.

The funeral service was nearly over when Paul Smith urged everyone present to be ready for that unknown hour when Christ comes or calls. Early in the service, his daughter (and Wesley's boyhood friend) Jan had sung her grandfather's, Dr. Oswald J. Smith's, hymn of comfort, "God Understands Your Sorrows."

"And now," Dr. Paul announced, "Let's all stand and sing."

> When the trumpet of the Lord shall sound,
> And time shall be no more,
> And the morning breaks, eternal, bright and fair;
> When the saved of earth shall gather
> Over on the other shore,
> And the roll is called up yonder, I'll be there.

It was the theme song of the boys' album, "Trumpets of the Lord."

Dr. Smith then performed the committal service right there in the church. It was the choice of the two families. Another service was certainly more than I could have handled. The good-byes in the vestibule were to us what to the world of nature would be like tearing a giant oak tree out of one's front garden. I then escorted Kathleen back to that special room, carefully facing her away from the window. Russell Wells, one of the closest friends we've ever had, provided a beautiful reception with refreshments afterward in the Fellowship Hall, but neither Kathleen nor I was strong enough to attend.

Instead, a long procession of the world's most sensitive friends of the bereaved came and poured into Kathleen and me the Balm of Gilead. Meanwhile, I stood facing the window, watching the casket being lifted into the hearse by big, strong Dan Southern and Wes's five other pallbearer friends. As it wended at a snail's pace out into Shepherd Avenue and westward toward Yonge, I felt my heart break apart, and I thought again of God giving His only begotten Son. The difference was, He did it willingly. We surrendered Wes with grieving, stubborn reluctance.

Having passed for those seconds of pause through death valley, I managed somehow to look to the mountain beyond, to seize upon those words still swirling around in my mind, "When the trumpet of the Lord shall sound," to match them with the penultimate verse of Scripture where Jesus assured the aged John, "Surely I am coming quickly." And I responded with John of old, "Amen. Even so, come, Lord Jesus!" And suddenly I realized, in contrast to the young man I've always imagined myself to be, that I too was an old man looking forward to that final glad day when we would be going up there to be forever with the Lord—and with Wes.

CHAPTER SIX

*T*he funeral over and Wes carried away in a shiny brown box pushed into the back of a gleaming black hearse, the crowd eventually dispersed and we went home, our boys handling us with the sensitivity my grandmother used to handle her Wedgwood china. They knew how fragile we were. There were so many people in our house that night, and the phone rang off the hook. And there was so much food. Bereaved people, I'm told, eat far too little or far too much. Kathleen called it comfort food. We ate it mostly because when we ate, it meant family or friends were with us.

When we got the news that Wes was killed, I didn't want to see anybody—not even myself in the mirror. From the funeral onward, the fear of being alone seized both Kathleen and me. Close friends and loved ones had a narcotic effect on us. We hated to see them get up from a meal table and leave; we would cling to them like leeches. Alone, I would brood, Kathleen would cry, all the while kissing various pictures of Wes. And I would hear her saying over and over again, "My son, Wesley! My son, Wesley!"

Kathleen's best comforts were the Lord and her three Irish sisters. They feathered our nest every day for weeks. When I was due to start a large, area-wide Crusade in Tucson, Arizona, on the Saturday two days after the funeral, we had a family discussion. Paul had to re-

turn the next week to Baylor and Bill the next month to
Thailand. Should I go? We decided I should. That's
what Wes would have wished. He believed totally in
what I was doing. I felt about as much like going as
Jonah felt initially about going to Nineveh. But Kathleen
had her sisters and two of the boys. I delayed one day,
but that sad, sad Sunday the planes on which I flew
seemed to be going the speed of an early nineteenth century wagon train.

Seated alone in a row of seats, I felt the Lord giving
me the sermon I should preach that night. It would be
John 3:16! What did God the Father give when He sent
His only begotten Son? I wrote out my notes on the two
sides of a 6 x 8 inch card. Not since the first century
have we known factually so well to what God the Father
was giving His Son. Writers who lived in the first century A.D., augmented by recent archaeological digs, have
been revealing more and more about the gruesomeness
and cruelty of Roman crucifixion. It had evolved over
the span of several centuries with the help of specialists
in the techniques of torture and terrorism. The savagery
of Jesus Christ's crucifixion was indescribable. No exe-
cution in all history could remotely compare with the
combined physical, mental, and spiritual anguish endured
by the Son of God on that blackest of days.

When Pontius Pilate turned Jesus over to the Roman
centurion and his company of Assyrian mercenary soldiers, they scourged Jesus mercilessly with a cat-o'-nine-
tails, which had nine leather thongs each studded with
razor-sharp blades of bone, metal, and jagged glass. The
soldiers competed with each other as if in a sporting
event and lashed His back thirty-nine times. At that
point, the centurion stepped forward and called an abrupt

halt before they broke through the rib cage and into His heart, which would spell instant death. They then hauled Him to the armory where a crown of thorns shaped like a skullcap was rammed onto His head. Those thorn bushes were unique to ancient Palestine; each thorn was four inches long, strong as a nail, needle-sharp with fish-hook-like points.

They then tore out whole clumps of His beard until His face was raw. They punched His cheeks with brass-knuckled fists. They put a mock scepter in His hand, then wrenched it loose, and with it beat Him over the head. They placed on His back a 110-pound crossbeam and prodded Him toward Calvary. He fell and they kicked Him to His feet, as a bypassing Cyrenian was recruited to carry His cross.

On Calvary's hill they stripped Him naked, screamed blasphemies into His ears, and before an upgazing howling mob, nailed His palms with rusty spikes—likely pulled the day before from a villain's hands—to the crossbar. Then, with a rope blood-soaked from previous use tied around the middle of the crossbar, they hoisted Him jerkily up a shorn tree and hung Him between two thieves.

They buckled His knees and drove the biggest spike through His two affixed feet, because death by crucifixion was induced by asphyxiation. The muscles of His chest were under incessant pressure. Every pain-shooting breath meant diminishing oxygen and a consequent build-up of lethal carbon dioxide, which issued in increasing cramps leading to violent convulsions. It was all deliberately contrived to warn any would-be breakers of Roman law what awaited defiant violators.

But what made the excruciating physical pain of the crucified's death unique was the fact that Romans invariably poured into the mouths of those they crucified an intoxicating brew that anesthetized their brains so that they had greatly reduced awareness of what was happening to them. Jesus rejected the offer, for He must suffer the full consequences of the world's guilt.

But it was the Father/Son relationship that I would be emphasizing: that it was the Father who sent the Son to be the Savior of the world. So Jesus addressed the first of His seven cries to His Father: "Father, forgive them, for they do not know what they do." Later, midnight darkness at midday wrapped the world in a stygian shroud, and abandoned by God and man, the Son of God cried, "My God, My God, why have You forsaken Me?" He exclaimed, "It is finished!" Redemption was complete; the sins of all were atoned for, and it was finally, "Father, into Your hands I commend My spirit." The Father then pronounced His confirmation of His Son's work by shaking the world with an earthquake. His Son had made atonement for the sins and souls of all mankind. His Father, with His only Son's sacrifice, was forever satisfied.

I would stress to that gathering that Kathleen and I surrendered Wes to death because we had no other choice. In my deepest grief I'd asked: "Where were You, God, when my son died?" Back had come His reply: "I was just where I was when My Son died!" God the Father "*gave* His only begotten Son, that whoever believes in Him should not perish but have everlasting life." Indeed everyone in that commodious arena could be saved if they so chose.

Getting off the last leg of the flight into Tucson, I experienced as welcoming a red carpet as I have ever seen. I found myself stumbling between two stools— their magnanimous reception and my reluctance. The crowd, too, was unbelievably sympathetic. I was shivering in my shoes, and my knees were knocking as they had not since I began preaching in my teens. As I got up to speak, dressed in black, my face, I am sure, was as pale as my name. I admitted outright that I would rather be in heaven than in Tucson, but I would try to preach, as best I could. Mingling with my irrepressible tears were sweat drops that seemed to be breaking out all over my body. It kept crossing my mind that Jesus, in the Garden of Gethsemane, sweated great drops as He sighed in consummate resignation, "Father, if it is Your will, remove this cup from Me; nevertheless not My will, but Yours, be done."

Richard Greene wrote of that service in *Decision* magazine (December 1991) to its several million readers, "With great emotion in his voice Dr. White . . . implored those attending to consider the finality of life on earth and the glories of eternal life in heaven. 'If there's an iota of doubt that you are totally Christ's, fully forgiven, completely accepted by God our heavenly Father through Christ alone, commit your life to Him. This is an hour of decision, a time of choice.' "

The number responding that night were two or three times as many as normal. One who gave his life to Christ in that service was the local sheriff, who had under his command 1,250 police and immigration control officers. He later wrote me a long, touching letter about the movement of God's Holy Spirit in his life that evening and about his surrender to Christ. That Thursday morning I joined him at six o'clock to walk up to a mountain and as the sun was rising, talk about the Son of God rising on the horizon of his life. He said he had been thinking constantly about that decision and living since in the wonder of Christ's reign of reality in his life.

Also attending that night's service and beginning that week with Christ was a Jewish realtor from New York. I, in retrospect, was grateful to God that I had made it clear in my address that it was not only the Jews who had nailed Jesus Christ, the Son of God, to the cross. It was every individual of every nation and generation, and that was why God gave His Son, that *whoever* believes in Him would have eternal life. That Jewish realtor believed, and the following Wednesday in an evangelical church, he gave a vibrant testimony of his coming to faith. The next Saturday at 9:30 P.M. he was killed in an automobile accident.

And there was an interesting conversation as our Team of seven assembled at the dinner table the next day. Kellye Cash, Miss America 1987 and grandniece of Johnny Cash, was our guest soloist and testifier for those first two nights. She had performed the same ministry for us earlier in the year in Shawnee, Oklahoma, at which time she told Kathleen and me that she was expecting her first baby. Might it be born on my birthday? I'd asked her. So now I asked her again: When was their boy born? It was on September 15, my birthday. It coincided with the last Sunday we had with Wes. I could not help but think of how close life and death are!

That week was extremely busy for me—Kiwanis, Lions, and Rotary; newspaper, TV, and radio interviews; and meetings with university students and government leaders. And from the people who came up onto the platform after the Crusade meetings, I began to realize how many parents there are who have lost children in accidents, and how often heartbreak is the means by which the Lord speaks. Jesus Christ says in His Revelation, "I stand at the door and knock. If anyone hears My voice and opens the door, I will come in" (Rev. 3:20). Life is filled with "knocks," including some really "hard knocks," and to dismiss them as accidents of fate is to ignore the claims of Jesus Christ upon our lives.

Examining my notes, I noticed that during that week the most meaningful illustrations I used were ones of people converted in meetings in which Wes was a part of our Crusade Team. He sang with his brothers; played the trumpet, the trombone, the piano, and the guitar; and most recently provided multimedia for my preaching. There was Colin Clark in England, converted as one of 110 who came forward one night as a teenaged "Teddy boy." (Teddy boys in England were the predecessors of British hippies.) It was in the Ilford Town Hall during the summer of 1964. What drew him was the BBC-TV appearance of the boys singing:

> Are you weary, are you heavyhearted?
> Tell it to Jesus, tell it to Jesus!
> Are you troubled at the thought of dying?
> Tell it to Jesus, tell it to Jesus.
> For Christ's coming Kingdom are you sighing?
> Tell it to Jesus alone.

They sang it again that night and Colin, deciding for Christ, has since become a prominent pastor and more recently, a well-known evangelist.

I told of Mark and Carol, children about the same age as our boys, who came to hear them sing and play in

Worthington, Minnesota, in August 1966. With us was Ethel Waters, and perhaps she's teamed up with Wes again, singing Wes's favorite of her songs: "Where Jesus Is, 'Tis Heaven There." And it was there that the boys learned to water ski, and Kathleen nearly did. Mark and Carol both came forward and gave their lives to Christ. Mark today is a distinguished Presbyterian minister and Carol an accomplished concert pianist, who also serves as her church organist and choir director.

It was in Duncan, Oklahoma, in August 1967, that our poodle Fred got lost. Its having been announced on the local radio station, someone triumphantly found him. But the highlight of that Crusade, as of all those we conducted, were the hundreds of spiritually lost people who were found. One of those nights, David Davis, an all-American, all-star high-school football player (the best in the nation at his position) came forward to surrender his life to Christ, and, we learned this summer, David has become a prominent Baptist pastor and evangelist in Houston. I shared that testimony with Wes over a meal, just a few days before his departure for heaven.

And I told him, too, about Mike Fischer, described by a Billy Graham Team member to me earlier this year as the finest evangelical musician in the upper Midwest. Where had he been converted prior to his going to Drake University and the Boston Conservatory of Music? He had believed as a farm boy in Mason City, Iowa, in 1977, at one of our Crusades, when Wes was showing his multimedia slides on the giant screen, and it was my privilege to be simultaneously preaching the gospel.

In 1978 there was Allan Trott, commander of the world's largest Air Force base, in California. (En route to that Crusade, in a leased Cessna 182, Wes and I almost went to heaven together, as near Eureka, California, a sudden massive fog descended without warning. As Wes did not yet have his instrument rating, it seemed to me a miracle that we didn't crash. It was the Lord's will and Wes's innate skill that saved us.)

Allan Trott was not in the habit of attending church, let alone a Billy Graham Associate Crusade. But the previous week he had been in touch daily with the White House and the Pentagon because of tensions in the Middle East. Also that week—and this was the crisis that brought him to the Crusade—he had been aboard the world's largest airplane, the C-5, when its wheels seized up, and his pilots circled for eleven hours, which included in-air refueling. He wrote later in a letter how in desperation he got down on his knees aboard that military mega-plane and prayed, "Father, God, if there is a God and You will let me have my feet safe on mother earth again, I will respond to Your call, whatever it may be."

So that Sunday night, with Wes handling the multimedia presentation on the second coming of Christ, Allan Trott and his family were in the Crusade in the front row. At the invitation Allan and his family came forward and gave their lives to Christ. A few weeks later, in Brazil, I received a beautiful letter of testimony from Allan. He was beginning his staff meetings each morning with prayer, because he reasoned that in such trying times as these, only the Lord could keep us on the path of His will.

I got home from those Crusades in Brazil early in the morning. During the night the McCanns's house, not one hundred yards from ours, had burned. Close friends of Wes, six of the family had perished. Mrs. McCann had gotten out, but young Sean was behind a wall of flames, so she had gone back through the firestorm, thrown Sean out through a window, then had herself perished. The clergyman at the funeral, standing behind those six coffins, took for his text John 15:13: "Greater love has no one than this, than to lay down one's life for his friends." Wes, Kathleen, and I were in the back pew. As the procession of coffins went by, Sean was following the last one—that of his mother. He turned and said to us, crying and pointing to the coffin, "She died for me!"

Wes was deeply moved. It was on the eve of Billy Graham's last Crusade in Toronto. Billy himself was deeply touched when I told it to our team gathering in a devotional and later in an address to the one thousand ministers and their wives assembled for the School of Evangelism. Billy used it one evening in his sermon in Maple Leaf Gardens as an illustration of Christ's dying on the cross that we might live. Wes's job during that Crusade was to record the twenty-five or more sermons given in that School of Evangelism. Perhaps Gabriel recorded them in heaven, and it's possible he and Wes are right now playing back Wes's favorites.

Tucson was undoubtedly the hardest Crusade for me ever to preach. But it was also a most blessed one. My life verse is Philippians 3:10: "that I may know Him and the power of His resurrection, and the fellowship of His sufferings." Both "the power of His resurrection and the fellowship of His sufferings" were Christ's abundant manifestation in my life that week!

CHAPTER SEVEN

After Tucson came back-to-back Crusades in Yuma, Arizona, the Imperial Valley in California, and Wilkes Barre, Pennsylvania. Kathleen came with me to the middle two, after which we spent several days with Paul in Waco, Texas. We learned a lot about bereavement, including the fact that there is just no way of blocking it out of your mind. There are those times of hilarious laughter, when someone you love or just like lingers over a slow breakfast and has the gift of humor. But alas, before we would get back to the room I might, without warning, start brooding again, going into what Winston Churchill called the "black dog" of depression, or what the more saintly John Wesley labeled my "wilderness journeyings." I simply could not fight off the episodes of mourning, so I resigned myself to living with them.

Kathleen could have the most delightful fellowship with this Jewish Christian, that pastor or doctor or farmer's wife, and she would think she was out of the woods for good. Then boom! That wave of weeping would come over her and there just wasn't anything to do but accept it, asking the Lord to heal.

C. S. Lewis said that the death of a family member was not like a wound that would heal. It was more like an amputated arm that you kept feeling was still there at your side. Your loved one is like that, no longer physically at your side, but somehow, mysteriously still with you.

One day in the Imperial Valley in California, Kathleen and I had one of those real downers—like we were playing Ping-Pong against a curb. I had no additional meetings, such as a Rotary Club or a TV interview. We just seemed all day to be blue without a break. Kathleen kept yearning for Wes to walk in "here" where we were, and I kept wishing we could walk in "there"—where he is. Prayer, studying the Word, talking to our close friends—nothing seemed to snap the spell. Then came the Crusade service. I was dreading it, rather than joyfully anticipating it. Suddenly Tom Bledsoe led us in a chorus about Jesus' being alive, and since He was indeed risen from the dead, Kathleen and I realized we would be able to face all our tomorrows because Christ was always with us.

Perhaps the loneliest I have ever felt was the Thursday afternoon we were in Wilkes Barre, Pennsylvania. Kathleen was at home. Paul was in Texas, Bill in Thailand, and Randy talking to his mother about flying again. She called and told me about it. He had not piloted an airplane of any kind since flying Wes's Comanche to New York and back two days before Wes's death. I got down on my knees to pray and prepare a sermon for that night, which would be shown later across Canada and the northern United States. From Alaska it would reach Russia, the country to which, God willing, we would be going the following month.

As I opened the Bible, all I could think of was Wes. As Sandra, his wife, emphasized, he had been becoming more and more careful as a pilot. In his training to become a commercial airline pilot, she stressed, he became extremely strict about adhering meticulously to the rigid rules to which every flyer at the controls of an airplane must commit him- or herself. Although they may well exist, I never met one of his flying colleagues who didn't tell me that Wes was the most capable, natural pilot they had ever been airborne with. It was their perception that, as he could handle anything with wheels, so he could handle anything with wings, even in the most critical emergencies. *Why, on September 28, did his right engine fail at a height that no pilot on earth could do anything about? Why, God?* That afternoon in Wilkes Barre it hit me like a ton of bricks. I felt so terribly alone.

Then, pondering the Scriptures in desperate quest, I came to this passage in 2 Corinthians 12:2–4 where the apostle Paul described his experience "in Christ . . . whether in the body, I do not know, or whether out of the body I do not know, God knows—such a one was caught up to the third heaven . . . and heard . . . words, which it is not lawful for a man to utter." I found myself on this basis, fantasizing, by faith, that I was up there with Wes. I had spent hundreds of hours flying hundreds of thousands of miles around the first heaven with him, and every minute, at least in retrospect, was joy unspeakable. Maybe, I thought, right now I could have a little talk about the good times I'd shared with him, say, here on earth in the "first heaven," and up there where he now was, in the "third heaven."

So that night while I was preaching I got to the point late in my sermon at which I was dealing with death and heaven. And I found myself dialoguing with Wes along the lines of my afternoon ruminations. These thoughts became the remainder of my address.

"Wes, do you remember when your Great-Grandmother Calderwood died? There was a Plymouth Brethren burial in Belfast. You and Bill insisted, even though you were only three years old, on coming to the cemetery with me. When they lowered the coffin, it was raining. Somehow you got loose from my hand and sauntered over to the grave. As you looked in, you slipped, and I grabbed you barely in time to keep you from falling in.

"A few days later our canary died. You, Bill and Paul came out to the back garden to bury it. You had in mind the burial service of your great-grandmother, and how your Grandpa Calderwood pronounced the final benediction at the committal, 'In the name of the Father, and of the Son, and of the Holy Ghost.' So when we buried the bird, as Bill dropped it into the hole you said, 'In the name of the Father, and of the Son, and into-the-hole-he-goes!' Do you remember that?

"Wes, do you remember the night in Titchfield in England in the big tent, when I was preaching? That too was when you were three and you thought I had spoken long enough. A pooch wandered into the tent and headed straight for you. Neither Bill nor Paul ever admitted that they dared you to do it. Anyway, you gave his tail one terrific twist. He took to barking, and that certainly sped the windup of that meeting!"

Wes always had that vicarious look of recollection and appreciation on his face. He never looked deadpan or bored. He was as an absorbing a listener as he was a talker and storyteller. And I envisaged him being as good a listener in heaven as he had been on earth.

"And do you remember the night you and Bill were awarded the B.A. from Richmond College? How I, as chancellor, conferred the degrees? But you and Bill never did give your dad the credit. You always told people that it was a Jerry Falwell thing, because he gave the convocation address that night. Actually your Uncle

Hugh as president was the one you owe most to. You made it.

"And Wes, do you remember about three years ago, just after Ben Johnson ran the one hundred meters faster than any person in the history of sport, at the Tokyo Olympics? And then the next week the man who *USA Today* said was, for a weekend, the most famous man in the world, became the most infamous. Ben had been on steroids and was found out. And it came out in the media that the whole Johnson family was crestfallen. Leighton Ford's son, Sandy, whom you had taken for a thrill ride over Niagara Falls in that Cessna 182, had been a runner. After Sandy's death, Leighton had written a book on Sandy's life. He thought it might be of help to Ben, so he called and wondered if I could take it out to Ben's home in east Toronto.

"So I asked you how to get to the Johnson home. You knew exactly where it was. You knew Ben. You had flown him to Montreal for a race. So you took me. Ben's sister, Dezrene, met us at the door. She burst into tears. She said that the previous Sunday morning their family had been terribly depressed. She had come to The People's Church, where I was preaching on Matthew 5:23, 'Bring your gift to the altar!' You were there that morning, Wes! And Dezrene had come forward and given her life to Christ. So she brought us in and assembled the family. You and I made a presentation of Leighton's book to Ben. Then we all knelt down and prayed. The only one who didn't kneel was Ben.

"And do you remember the year we had the championship hockey team at Richmond? You had gotten hooked on hockey ten years earlier as a little tyke. Your father was playing for Oxford against Cambridge in England. It was the first time you ever saw a hockey game. Cricket, soccer, rugby, football, basketball, baseball—from then on you reckoned that when compared with hockey, they were as a Corvair to a Corvette. It was so fast, so flashy, so suspense-filled. For the rest of your life, there was just no matchup of wits and skills like it.

"You remember Cambridge beat us, 7 to 3, that night and also broke Peter Dawkins's leg, and I helped carry him off. Later, Peter, as a U.S. Army General, became a war hero in Vietnam and in the '80s was touted by *Time* as a potential candidate for the presidency of the United States.

"Anyway, you guys really practiced—hours every week—that year. As your coach, it was my highest hope to take you down to Chicago to play Wheaton College, from which I had graduated in 1952. You remember some of our other players couldn't come because of work schedules so your little brother, Randy, and two cousins, Donald and Charles, who hadn't grown up yet either, came.

"Wes, that was the day you had the caps of your two front teeth knocked off by a highstick in an afternoon game against Trinity College in Deerfield, Illinois. You won thirteen to one. You didn't seem to care about the teeth thing, just so you won! Wes, somewhere someone like you may exist, but I have never known anyone, anywhere, who enjoyed winning so much, but hated as much as you to lose anything.

"And to think that with just eleven players, three of them little squirts, you had the energy to take on vaunted Wheaton in the evening. It was crazy. You remember that Dr. Basil Jackson came from Milwaukee. A psychiatrist who headed a team of nineteen other psychiatrists, he had been on our "Agape" television team with Bev Shea, Evie Tornquist, Stephan Tchividjian, and Millie Dienert. He was also an Irishman, like you guys. Before taking the ice, we had gone over the game plan to score early and hang on, having only eleven players, and your second game that day. Basil led the prayer: 'God, You know these fellas are being coached by the chancellor. He's so anxious to win this game that if these guys don't, he won't give any of them a B.A. degree. Amen!'

"Do you remember my telling you about Gill Dodds? He was the world champion indoor miler and our track coach when I was at Wheaton. Harv Crouser was his colleague. And Mr. Crouser was still there when I brought you guys back. When he saw the three little guys in the pre-game skate, he came over and said to me, 'John, we follow you around here in your work as a Billy Graham evangelist and we know you from speaking in chapel. But those little guys . . . the crowd is big tonight and we have on our team some rather rough football players from Minnesota, Michigan, and Massachusetts. They can be tough along the boards, playing hockey, and I would ask you not to play those little fellas. I don't think there's insurance to cover them if they are not *bona-fide* college students.'

"I was on the spot. I was so anxious to win that game that I could taste it. I replied, 'Mr. Houser, I'm really in a bind. Several of our players couldn't come, so rather than cancel, I . . .'

" 'Okay, John, but they'll have to play at your own risk.' Mr. Crouser then positioned himself straight across the rink from our bench and watched me like a hawk. The opening face-off took place. I was as nervous as a cat on a hot tin roof.

"I sent all non-Whites out for the first shift, to face their best. Wheaton's biggies backed our guys into our own end, and you may remember, it looked as if we were in big trouble. And then for the second shift, Wes, I sent you out to right wing, Paul at center, little Randy on left wing, with Bill and little Donald on defense. Even before the puck was dropped, you fellas looked as if you were about to be shot out of a cannon. Your mother had put big white letters on each of your jerseys, and it was obvious to all who weren't blind that you were Whites. We had that play thoroughly rehearsed in advance. Would it work? I wondered for a minute if we were in over our heads this time. You guys had never lost a game in the United States. This might be the first.

"Paul skated into the center of the circle to the left of our goalie. He won the face-off and snapped the puck through his legs to Randy behind him, who backhanded a pass around the backboards to Donald. He headmanned it through a Wheaton defenseman's legs to Bill, who one-handed a pinpoint pass to you. You reached behind you and pulled the puck forward in your skates, barely on side, streaking like greased lightning over the blue line. You were in full flight, all right.

"Wheaton's biggest defenseman was backing up frantically and you did that hot-dogging sweep around, holding him at arm's length with your left elbow. The whole crowd came to its feet as you put on an exhibition of how to beat a goalie one-on-one, deeking him over to the left side of the net and then, in close, burying the puck with a bullet to the top right-hand corner. You savored nothing more than to see the goal-judge turn on that red light. As you wheeled around with your stick up over your head—Gordie Howe style—you flashed a glance back to the coach on the Richmond bench. His buttons were about to break, he was so ecstatic.

"Billy Graham's daughter Gigi and son-in-law, Stephan, told me that the whole crowd was awestruck, silent as a tomb. John Dillon was nearly grinning his cheeks off. He had come all the way from Minneapolis, as Gigi and Stephan had come from Milwaukee, just to see you play. They were the only supporters you guys had in that crowd that night, except, of course, your mother and both poodles, who barked up a storm. Being from Britain, your mother may not have known much more about hockey than a jackrabbit knows about Ping-Pong, but she was definitely cheering for the White boys.

"As the red light flashed, I looked across the ice surface, and Harv Crouser was staring at me quizzically. I allowed myself a half grin, a wink, and a hand gesture, in which my index finger did a half curl and connected with my thumb. I aimed it at Mr. Crouser. I think he got the message.

"Wes, I have to say that in my whole life, that was the most gratifying gesture I ever performed in sports, as my fatherly ego for a moment inflated to approximately the size of Manhattan. You went on, as I recall, to score five goals in an 11 to 6 win. But, boy, with as few players on the bench as we had, were you guys ever bushed when the horn went, ending the game!

"You know, Wes, I told that story at a meal table later where Wheaton's president, Hudson Armerding, and Billy Graham were present. Billy loved it, but Dr. Armerding hated it. He was at the game. He was a saint as he was a scholar. But he, like Harv Crouser, didn't ever like to see Wheaton lose.

"Wes, you and I were supposed to be flying up next month to Cape Dorset for a Crusade for Christ with the Inuits. What happened when that twin Comanche crashed? Had they put bad fuel in your tanks? All the experts I have talked to tell me that when a motor fails on a twin at under a hundred feet, there's not a thing any pilot can do. And, Wes, your mother and I have kept wondering—like nearly all the time—did it hurt?"

That was as far as I could get that night preaching in Wilkes Barre. Like walking down the aisle of People's Church for Wes's funeral, I lost it. So after seconds of choked-up silence, I just gave the invitation to those who felt their need to come forward to Christ if they wanted to go to heaven. There was an avalanche.

CHAPTER EIGHT

*T*he precious things of heaven!" (Deut. 33:13). Moses saved this description for the penultimate of the 187 chapters of the Scriptures attributed to his authorship. It was immediately prior to his ascent, at the age of 120, to Mount Nebo. At the top was the peak, Pisgah, from which he would take a look at the whole of the promised land, then depart from earth for his eternal home in heaven. He would prove his immortality by his reappearance on the Mount of Transfiguration, talking with Elijah and Jesus (Matt. 17:3).

There are 697 scriptural references to heaven. That's a very great number. I had an interest in heaven previous to September 28, but it was the heaven to which believers would arise at the return of Christ. It never occurred to me to study or think much about the heaven which is the present residence of departed believers in the Lord Jesus Christ. Such a heaven, to me, was a state of ethereal existence in which the saints of the past were in a holding pattern. I never concerned myself much about whether or not they were engaged in floating around on a cloud, waiting for the real eternity to begin when the rest of us arrived. I took it for granted that the real game had not yet begun. The first pitch had not yet been thrown. The kick-off was yet future. The opening face-off with the great forever was still to come.

What a dimension of Christian reality I was missing! Heaven, in the present, for departed believers, is a real place for real people who have sublimely heightened consciousness and immensely increased knowledge. They are engaged in greatly enhanced activity and are free of all pain or tension in an environment of perpetual, celestial bliss. Suddenly, because Wes was there, I found myself concentrating my thinking, whenever my mind was sufficiently free from work pressures to do so, on what heaven was like.

Even with all the responsibilities I was carrying, the Billy Graham Team members with whom I hold Crusades could not help but be aware that I seemed to be periodically absentminded, daydreaming a lot, and making a lot of mistakes. My subconscious mind seemed constantly to be preoccupied with what it was really like up there in heaven, where Wes now lived and moved and had his being.

I recall how Billy Graham, in that New York area Crusade in September immediately prior to Wes's death, told with great emotion about standing as a young preacher at his dying grandmother's bedside. A day before she died she was seeing and talking with her late husband, Ben. It was clear he was with Christ, living in a state of ideal, unbroken joy. That point was doubtless extraordinarily touching to many, but it didn't especially move me as I sat behind Billy on the platform watching the TV monitor. But when that sermon was shown on television earlier this month, I found myself reflecting on it over and over. *Was it possible that Wes, with Christ as he is, could be as communicative to us in our grief and expectation as Billy's grandfather was to his grandmother?*

And there was also Billy's sister, Jean Ford. Kathleen and I spoke several times with both Jean and Leighton on the telephone. News that Jean had communicated, however briefly, with Sandy had great meaning for Kathleen and me. Leighton, with his wonderful mind, likened communication with departed loved ones to changing channels on a television set—those who have gone on to heaven being on a channel, however, to which we don't normally have access. One day we will.

And then there was the day in Rochester, New York, in October when Esther and Sterling Huston sat with Kathleen and me over a breakfast that led up to lunchtime. Esther told us about her aged dad, whom she had attended the day before his death. He asked her, "Is Mark coming again?" Recognizing that he had seen her brother, who had been killed overseas a full generation earlier during World War II, Esther reassured him, "Yes, he is coming soon."

Kathleen and I hung on every word. I was, there and then, nearly overwhelmed with the desire to go and be with the Lord and with Wes. *They would be such marvelous company,* I kept telling myself.

But just where is Wes? The apostle Paul taught unequivocally that he is with Christ and all the saints of the ages. Paul's statement reads, "We are confident." Indeed, as believers in Christ we have an indisputable preference to be "absent from the body and to be present with the Lord" (2 Cor. 5:8). Paul himself had the perpetual "desire to depart and be with Christ, which is far better" (Phil. 1:23). He was no manic-depressive for whom human existence on earth was a drudgery. He was a rejoicer! For him "to live is Christ," anywhere in this world, regardless of how adverse the circumstances. But "to die is gain" (Phil. 1:21). What he meant was that life after death was a far fuller existence, because "now we see in a mirror, dimly, but then face to face. Now I know in part, but then I shall know just as I also am known" (1 Cor. 13:12).

So for us, his family, to yearn, dream, or even fantasize that Wes may come back for a while, is not wrong. But, from Wes's present vantage point, for him to return to this temporal, terrestrial world would be unthinkable. It is not that no one ever has. Moses, Samuel, Elijah, Elisha, the lads whom Elijah and Elisha respectively witnessed being raised from the dead, the son of the widow of Nain, the daughter of Jairus, Lazarus, the uncounted saints on the day of Jesus' crucifixion, Dorcas, and Eutychus all came back from the dead.

But the only saint who—after his death, in words that we have recorded in the Bible—spoke to us was the prophet Samuel. King Saul, having been on the throne of Israel forty years, had latterly, in his own words, "played the fool." He was in big trouble. So he, through the woman of En Dor, invoked Samuel to come back, which Samuel did with the utmost reluctance. Samuel complained to Saul, "Why have you disturbed me by bringing me up?" His would be a truly terrifying message. Samuel soberly told Saul he would die: "Tomorrow you and your sons will be with me" (1 Sam. 28:14–19).

Saul was terror-stricken, falling and groveling on the ground. But for Saul to argue or protest was useless. The next day the Philistines slaughtered Saul's sons, Abinadab and Melchishua, and also Jonathan. Saul, with his sons dead as Samuel, the prophet, had promised, ran on his own sword. The four bodies, bloodied by death, returned to the ground as dust to dust. But their spirits, their personalities, the real Saul, Jonathan, Melchishua, and Abinadab, had departed to be with the Lord, joining Samuel. Their bodies were indeed dead, but they lived on as spiritual persons, as their great teacher Moses assured, "The eternal God is your refuge, and underneath are the everlasting arms" (Deut. 33:27).

Wes's spirit is the real and immortal Wes. The apostle James clarified that though Wes's natural "body without the spirit is dead" (2:26), his spirit lives on, not as a mere memory for us to recall, but as the forever-living personality which is the true Wes. Solomon the wise wrote to his sons, reminding us how Wes "goeth to his long home, and the mourners [we here] go about the streets . . . [as Wes's] spirit [has returned] unto God who gave it" (Eccl. 12:5, 7 KJV).

Jesus Christ, through His atonement on the cross, became "a life-giving spirit" (1 Cor. 15:45). In this capacity, He became Wes's Savior and gave him eternal life. So from the time he gave himself to Jesus Christ as a boy, the "Spirit [of the Lord bore] witness with [Wes's] spirit that [he was one of the] children of God" (Rom. 8:16). So Wes's spirit having become God's (1 Cor. 6:20) stations him today "in the heavenly places in Christ Jesus" (Eph. 2:6), vitally "joined to the Lord [in] one spirit" (1 Cor. 6:17)!

In having departed from this life, Wes joined in heaven "the spirits of just men made perfect" (Heb. 12:23). Like his father, he wasn't perfect on this earth. Nor was Paul "already perfected" (Phil. 3:12) prior to his death. But both Paul and Wes are "made perfect" now. That Saturday afternoon when Wes went to be with the Lord, he yielded himself to "the Father of spirits" (Heb. 12:9).

The evening before His crucifixion, our Lord's body was near exhaustion, as in the Garden of Gethsemane He lamented, "The spirit indeed is willing, but the flesh is weak" (Matt. 26:41). The day following, His spirit departed from His body at the moment of His death. On the third day, His body was resurrected as a result of His spirit rejoining His body. Earlier when Jesus had raised Jairus's daughter from the dead, Doctor Luke explained, "her spirit returned" (8:55) and united with her body, after which she lived a normal life.

So Wes is with Christ. Longing as we are to see him, I would not wish him back. He loved the multidimensional life. That's why he rode those fast motorcycles, loved watching car races, and flew airplanes high in the sky. The first chapter of Ezekiel never meant much to me until now. Ezekiel describes how to him "the heavens were opened, and I saw visions of God." Up there were beings with "four wings . . . and they sparkled like the colour of burnished brass. . . . Whither the spirit was to go, they went . . . as the appearance of a flash of lightning. [They could actually spin] one wheel upon the earth [but, as they sped at or above the speed of lightning—which is 186,000 miles per second] [the wheels'] appearance . . . was as it were a wheel in the middle of a wheel. When they went, they went upon their four sides" (1:1, 6, 7, 12, 14–17 KJV). I can just see Wes up there, perhaps behind that wheel in the middle of a wheel, winging it all around heaven.

If he were to land his UFO in our backyard, he would definitely have difficulty getting his mother aboard. I never declined his offer, however, while he was here on earth, to go for a spin on or in any vehicle he controlled. And if I thought he were coming in for a landing this minute, I would drop this pen, pronto, and be out there eager to take off.

When David Frost interviewed Billy Graham on PBS, he asked what Billy expected the Lord to have him do when he died and went to heaven. Billy replied that Revelation 22:3, amidst a marvelous description of heaven, states that Christ's "servants shall serve Him." So Billy would aspire perhaps to go from planet to planet where living souls may reside and there preach to them the everlasting gospel. It made me think: Then possibly I could be there, as I am here, his Associate Evangelist, and Wes could pilot me from place to place, spreading the good news that Jesus Christ is Lord over all things, in heaven as on earth.

But does Wes have a body now in which his spirit resides? I believe he does. The apostle Paul wrote to the Corinthians—in present tense—"There is a natural body, and there is a spiritual body" (1 Cor. 15:44). Philippians 3:21 says there will be a glorified body at the time of Christ's return. This is what Paul wrote about when he wanted us to "know that if our earthly house, this tent [the natural body], is destroyed, we have a building from God" [a spiritual body]. "For in this we groan." Wes's most grievous groan was doubtless that fateful Saturday afternoon in September, even more travailing than when he was born in Belfast. Believers on this earth, because of the tears, sorrow, and suffering, are "burdened . . . because we want to be . . . clothed, that mortality may be swallowed up by life" (2 Cor. 5:1, 2, 4). If we are still alive when Christ comes back to take us home, the Lord Jesus Christ "will transform our lowly body that it may be conformed to His glorious body" (Phil. 3:20, 21). So Wes is in his "spiritual body" currently. At Christ's return, with the rest of us believers, he will be issued an eternal glorified body.

Obviously, when Jesus was here on earth, His disciples thought that for a person to be seen, he had to have a "natural body." One never-to-be-forgotten night en route across the Sea of Galilee, a ferocious storm descended. The apostles were terrified that their ship might capsize and sink. Jesus came walking to them on the water. On first seeing Him, they exclaimed, "It is a spirit" (Matt. 14:26 KJV). Later, when Jesus had died, risen, and suddenly appeared to them, "they were terrified and frightened, and supposed they had seen a spirit" (Luke 24:37). It is obvious from these and many other Scriptures that a person in a "spiritual body" can appear to humans to be natural bodies.

So might Wes speak or appear to his mother or me, with words of kindly comfort or counsel, some time soon? I'm not expecting him to do so, although as his mother goes nightly into our living room and kisses his pictures as she weeps, calls him by name, and talks to him as if he were still here, there are times I intensely wish he would.

But of this we can be sure. Wes is currently blooming. His time on earth, as Jesus said, was like that of a seed buried in the ground. He has now germinated. We used to say on our Saskatchewan wheat farm that in late spring, maybe two weeks after the crops were seeded, "Oh, look, it's coming up!" It meant that the stone-gray soil was sprouting an elegant coat of green grain. On September 28, Wes "came up." He ascended to heaven.

When he and I flew together, we would talk a lot. One day we got onto how a worm in a cocoon suddenly breaks out into a beautiful, skyborne butterfly. That's what happened to Wes. Here on earth he had an abundance of that thing called personality. In heaven, he now has personality with a capital "P."

His mind is developing to its fullest potential, as we read in Scripture that the process had only begun on earth. Whereas here Wes was "renewed in the spirit of [his] mind" (Eph. 4:23), up there the process is greatly accentuated. Wes's mind, with its present evolving capacity, is an integral part of his spirit. The ancient Job observed, "There is a spirit in man: and the inspiration of the Almighty giveth [Wes] understanding" (32:8 KJV). Jesus Himself is Wes's tutor, and consequently "the spirit [of Wes] knoweth" (1 Cor. 2:11 KJV) currently what no one ever on this earth knew, apart from Jesus Christ.

I take great consolation from Paul's final benediction as given in 2 Timothy 4:22: "The Lord Jesus Christ be with your spirit." From the moment Wes invited Jesus Christ into his life, our Lord assured him, He's "the same yesterday, today, and forever" and as such "will never, [it's a triple negative in the Greek—hence] no never, no never leave you nor forsake you" (Heb. 13:8, 5).

Some of us quote verses for years without realizing their meaning. For me, one of those was 1 Thessalonians 5:10. The previous verse assures us that "God did not appoint us to wrath, but to obtain salvation through our Lord Jesus Christ." It's the next verse that I didn't comprehend until Wes's death: Christ "died for us, that whether we wake or sleep, we should live together with Him." Living "with" Christ, Wes is incalculably more alive today than he was during that lively celebration of my last birthday.

Being with the Lord, Wes is constantly worshiping Jesus Christ around the throne of God and with all the saints of all the ages he's singing, "To Him who loved us and washed us from our sins in His own blood, and has made us kings and priests to His God and Father, to Him be glory and dominion forever and ever. Amen" (Rev. 1:5, 6).

When we lived in Oxford, we went to the seacoast at Exmouth, in the south of England, for meetings. Wes, as a small boy, was especially attentive to the account of a boy there, about his age, who was dying of leukemia. Moments before his death, he regained consciousness long enough to call out, "Bring!"—then fell back. His loving mother rushed out and brought him a square of his favorite Cadbury chocolate. He waved it off. Moments later, he called out again, "Bring!" His distraught father dashed to the kitchen and brought him a glass of water. Again, he shook his head. The third time he lifted himself up on his elbows, and focusing his eyes as if gazing right through the ceiling—not unlike the way the first martyr Stephen looked up into heaven when he was being stoned—the boy exclaimed, "Bring! Bring!" He was obviously trying to say more. Suddenly he exclaimed in his last words on earth, "Bring forth the royal diadem and crown Him Lord of all!" Angel arms then enfolded him home to where Jesus said of the young, "that in heaven their angels always see the face of My Father who is in heaven" (Matt. 18:10). For nearly twenty-five years Wes has been cheering the Toronto Maple Leafs, and all they've done is lose. Now He's worshiping a Winner.

CHAPTER NINE

What else is Wes doing in heaven with Jesus besides worshiping? Our Lord didn't leave us to guess. He said, "In My Father's house are many mansions; if it were not so, I would have told you. I go to prepare a place for you. And if I go and prepare a place for you, I will come again and receive you to Myself; that where I am, there you may be also" (John 14:2–3). So Jesus Christ is preparing places for us, and Wes, along with all the saints of all the ages, is up there "with Christ." I suspect that just as Jesus assigned tasks to His twelve disciples, He has all those believers whom He has called home functioning as a task force preparing those many mansions for the arrival of all the saints. Jesus is the "master builder," and as the "head contractor," He has a work for all departed saints to do.

Here on earth, Jesus was a carpenter. For three years He ministered, but for thirty years He built furniture and finished the internal upholstering of houses to make them happy homes. That's what He's doing in heaven, and Wes is working with Him. And just as Wes sought the acceptance and approval of his imperfect father (most of the time) here on earth, so he is doing with his perfect Lord in heaven. The apostle Paul made this unmistakably clear in 2 Corinthians 5:9, where he stated that once Wes was "present" with the Lord, he would "labour" to "be accepted" of Christ, just as obedient Christians here on earth "labour that we may be accepted of him" (KJV).

Here on earth Wes never had a lazy bone in his body. He was a hyperactive child and to the day of his death had boundless energy. He loved building. I have had many people tell me that his Eskimo Art Gallery was the most exotic and exquisite of its kind in Canada. And it was to build it up more elaborately that he embarked on that fateful September flight. Walking into his showroom down on Queen's Quay, you could see the rotating stands situated in every direction on which was mounted his huge, twenty-thousand-dollar falcon, his centerpiece, surrounded by muscular, gleaming polar bears; elegant caribou that roam the north in herds; regal eagles; massive walruses; slippery-looking seals; the loons aloft; the sly fox; the handsome husky dogs, all under the command of precisely-sculptured Eskimo people engaging in their sundry activities. It was, as a sight, a collector's dream.

A few nights ago, Dan Southern called me and asked, "Did you see Wes on Billy Graham's Christmas special on network television?" We had missed it, but I had just received the videotape in the mail, and we played it on our TV. Cliff Barrows was presiding. Sure enough, in the stable scene, preparing for the first coming of Jesus Christ, there was Wes, with a hammer in his hand, getting a place ready for the birth of Jesus. We played that part over and over again. And unfamiliar as I am with the tools of heaven, I cried; but I also cheered. Yes, what he so much loved doing down here, he's doing now, up there!

From the time he was tiny, he could assemble Tinkertoys better than any of the other boys. While I was at

Oxford, to keep the wolf off the doorstep we would buy three-hundred-year-old Shakespearean cottages, modernize them, and then resell them for a profit. Of our four boys, the one who was at my side most to wield shovel, pickax, hammer, saw, or screwdriver, was Wes. When he was eight years old, we were working on a pair of connected cottages in a place called Wootton, which involved going to and from on a remote country road. After bugging me a bit, he convinced me to teach him to drive. I remembered that on the Saskatchewan farm where I was born and brought up, I was driving by that age. He proved himself an immediate veteran as he looked under the upper rim of the steering wheel and barely over the low dashboard of that English Vauxhall. One day he "floor-boarded it," as I afterwards heard him brag to his brothers, hitting sixty-five miles per hour. He would drive any number of nails after that, if the reward was to drive that Vauxhall along that remote country road.

Wes was back at Oxford in the '80s with his mother and me during a Billy Graham mission to England. He had to see that cottage! So we drove up from London. When we knocked, no one was home, so we knocked on the door of the cottage across the street. An English woman, who was glad to talk, answered the door. She said that that particular cottage had just been resold by a shrewd realtor to a rather gullible young couple who were "culture vultures." The sale was on the basis that this particular cottage was one of historic significance because John Wesley had lived there. The price, therefore, was half as much again as it would have been, and the vendor collected every pound he asked. I knew, of course, that the great founder of Methodism had no more lived there than had Julius Caesar. But as Wes enjoyed telling the story, "The realtor had missed it by one. There had, in fact, been not one, but two John Wesleys who had lived there: John Wesley White, Sr., and John Wesley White, Jr.!"

When we moved to our present home in North York, Ontario, in 1966, Wes was a vigorous initiator of the idea that we should build a swimming pool in our backyard and at one end a high, wooden diving board. When finally we decided to do so in 1968, it meant going to the builder and buying the plumbing items. Wes was about five times as good at reading detailed plumbing instructions as he was at the "new math" at Zion Heights Junior High School. And to construct the wooden casing, behind which the concrete was poured, he was about twice as good at sawing the boards and driving in the nails as he was at writing an essay on why his trendy teacher thought Pierre Elliott Trudeau—having been sworn in that April—would make a good prime minister.

By fall, it was time to drain the swimming pool and build a cedar fence around the far backyard for an enclosed hockey rink! Once again, Wes generated the enthusiasm. Four-by-fours had to be set into the ground four feet deep. So we went to the rent-all at Finch and Yonge, and it was Wes who got the gasoline engine running to power the posthole digger. As we augured out the holes, he reckoned, "Dad, I'm just like you. I've earned my Ph.D.—I'm a Posthole Digger."

It was while Bill, Wes, and Paul were concurrently undergraduates in Richmond College that I served as chancellor. If Wes had to hit the books, he reasoned he would have to have a room more conducive for study. He, Randy, his mother, and I had been in Switzerland with Billy Graham for the initial Lausanne Conference on Evangelism. While there, he had taken a fancy to Bavarian decor. On our way back, we spent time in England, and he was attracted to Tudor-styled buildings with their wood-trim designs. I suspected, and I'm sure I was right, that his latest ploy had something to do too with reducing his study time!

So one Monday, when I arrived home from a Crusade in Greenwood, Indiana, there in his room was a tall pile of rough-hewn Black Forest spruce boards, which his cousin Kenneth got for him from huge wooden crates that an importer brought from Europe. His mother was sure they would bring woodworm into our house. I swallowed hard and said nothing. When Wes wanted something badly, he could really turn on the charm. Two or three hours a day, for three or four weeks, he would be up there sawing, hammering, working with a rented power screwdriver, and doing stuccowork. He got help from his cousin and long-time friend, Doug McVety, but none from his brothers.

Alas, when I returned from a Crusade in Cheyenne, Wyoming, Wes escorted me proudly up the stairs and into what was the last word, during those years, in Tudor Bavarian decor. On the walls were huge rough-wood-framed pictures of the latest Mossport and Indianapolis 500 championship winning cars with their drivers. And there were hockey trophies galore gleaming in chrome and crystal dust set against the rustic board walls. And he designed it so that the ceiling would light up like stars on an Australian night. The word in those days was "psychedelic." And stereos! He could get supersound out of the most twisted and gnarled ropes of flared wires I'd ever seen. It was a precursor of his Eskimo Art Gallery, and perhaps the crafting of his gallery was preparation for what Jesus has him doing in heaven right now.

When I open the Bible to Revelation and read descriptions of our eternal home, I haven't the slightest doubt that Wes is up there having a ball, and he's lending a hand in working alongside Jesus, shaping things to come. I think Jesus will put to maximum use his earthly expertise at laying out those spreads of precision-shaped, handcrafted Eskimo carvings in stone which so beautifully reflect the colors of the rainbow and the facial expressions that cross the whole gamut of temperaments.

In the past, I never could get myself to ponder Revelation 21, which describes what Wes is working on right now. But since he ascended, I'm reading it over and over. An angel invited John, the revelator, " 'Come, I will show you the bride, the Lamb's wife.' And he carried me away in the Spirit . . . and showed me the great city, the holy Jerusalem, [which in the future will be] descending out of heaven from God, having the glory of God. And her light was like a most precious stone, like a jasper stone, clear as crystal. [It] had a great and high wall with twelve gates . . . three gates on the east, three gates on the north, three gates on the south, and three gates on the west. . . . [And] he who talked with me had a gold reed to measure the city . . . [which] is laid out as a square. . . . Its length, breadth, and height are equal [1,500 miles each way]. . . . And the foundations of the wall of the city were adorned with all kinds of precious stones: the first foundation was jasper, the second sapphire, the third chalcedony, the fourth emerald, the fifth sardonyx, the sixth sardius, the seventh chrysolite, the eighth beryl, the ninth topaz, the tenth chrysoprase, the eleventh jacinth, and the twelfth amethyst. And the twelve gates were twelve pearls: each individual gate was of one pearl. And the street of the city was pure gold. . . . [And] the city had no need of the sun or of the moon to shine in it, for the glory of God illuminated it. The Lamb is its light" (Rev. 21:9–23).

Something that will especially please Wes: "Its gates shall not be shut at all by day (there shall be no night there." (v. 25). Wes never liked closed gates or closed doors, and he never liked the night.

So when I read Paul's words from 1 Thessalonians 2:19, I have a new appreciation for such affirmations as, "What is our hope, or joy, or crown of rejoicing? Is it not even you in the presence of our Lord Jesus Christ at His coming?"

I'm longing to see Christ at His coming. But now I'm longing also to see Wes; the look on his face, like when he had scored a winning goal in a tight hockey game, and he would always turn and look at the "gipper"; or when they had sung the last verse of "In the Sweet By and By" and they would reach up for those final climactic notes that said, "We shall meet on that beautiful shore!" and he would look over to where I was sitting just as the Crusade crowd burst into a protracted ovation.

Those looks, in retrospect, meant far more to the one being looked at than to the one who looked. It was as close to heaven as his father has ever been. And it's doubly why daily I pray with John's benediction at the end of the Bible, "Even so come, Lord Jesus!" To see Christ is paramount, but next comes my intense longing to see Wes. So in my moments alone, I quote over and over again, 1 Thessalonians 3:13, "Father, 'at the coming of our Lord Jesus Christ with all His saints,' please have

Wes close to the front so that I can see him right away!"
Jude 14 adds confirmation to those comforting words.
"Enoch, the seventh from Adam, prophesied. . . . 'Behold, the Lord comes with ten thousands of His saints.' "
One of those will be Wes!

So must Wes's death be considered his ultimate defeat? No, it was the occasion, instead, of his stepping into victory! Paul wrote to the Corinthians about it when he unveiled "a mystery: We shall not all sleep, but we shall all be changed—in a moment, in the twinkling of an eye, at the last trumpet. For the trumpet will sound, and the dead will be raised incorruptible. . . . For this corruptible must put on incorruption. . . . Then shall be brought to pass the saying that is written: 'Death is swallowed up in victory. O Death, where is your sting? O Hades, where is your victory?' . . . Thanks be to God, who gives us the victory through our Lord Jesus Christ" (1 Cor. 15:51–55, 57).

So where is Wes? He is among the redeemed with the Lord, among those to whom Hebrews 11:4 says, "He being dead still speaks," leading on to Hebrews 12:1–3 which promise, "Therefore we also, since we are surrounded by so great a cloud of witnesses [departed saints], let us lay aside every weight, and the sin which so easily ensnares us, and let us run with endurance the race that is set before us, looking unto Jesus, the author and finisher of our faith, who for the joy that was set before Him endured the cross, despising the shame, and has sat down at the right hand of the throne of God" (Heb. 12:1–2). Yes, heaven with its supernal reality is not merely waiting to happen at the taking home of the church, or after the millennium. It's in full swing right now.

EPILOGUE

For three months, our family has been through the valley of the shadow of death, a shadow, as the Bible states, of things to come. Nonetheless, this experience has been extremely painful. The Christmas to New Year's week had been a week in which in past years we celebrated not only the holidays but our wedding anniversary; and in one great party, the birthdays of Bill, Wes, and Paul. But alas, this December 28 is instead a commemoration of Wes's death. He's been in his "long home" three months.

I fly, some years, one hundred thousand miles. Those clouds! They're dark and foreboding from beneath. Once you soar above them, they're like a sea of silver in the golden celestial sunshine. So under the cloud of bereavement I have been down, but I've finally been down on my knees too, imploring: "Lord, it's time—wouldn't You say—for us to move on from this deep, debilitating grief to share a little of the healing, the wholeness that Wes is currently enjoying to the full in his departure to be with You?" So on December 28, three months after Wes's departure to be with Christ, I opened the Scriptures to 2 Kings, chapter 2. Getting up from prayer, I faced a pile of sympathy and Christmas cards. And I felt completely overwhelmed by the kindness of others and the grace of God, which is sufficient for every need. But

I also felt abysmally ashamed that we had been unable to muster the strength to send any season's greeting cards ourselves. So I sat down and penned a letter to those priceless friends and relatives who had communicated with us, and this is how it reads:

"You remembered Kathleen and me in the autumn of our grief, and we were deeply touched. We were not strong enough this season to send any Christmas cards, nor to celebrate Christmas at our home. His brothers, Kathleen and I have found it very hard to say good-bye to Wes. . . . We've struggled much more than we anticipated with the tears, anger, and unrealistic reluctance to let Wes go.

"But on the morning of December 28, Wes having been in his 'long home' three months, I was reading again from 2 Kings. Elijah was swept up to heaven in a whirlwind carried in a chariot of fire, powered by horses of fire, not unlike Wes's ascent. When Elisha returned to Jericho, the prophets insisted on sending fifty men to search the mountains and valleys in quest of Elijah. For three days they hunted, only to come back without finding him. Elisha rebuked them sharply for trying to bring back one whom the Lord had taken home.

"Did Elijah ever come back? Yes, with Jesus Christ to the Mount of Transfiguration—just as Wes will. For Paul wrote, 'Then we who are alive and remain shall be caught up together with them [those who, like Wes, are with Jesus] in the clouds to meet the Lord in the air. And thus we shall always be with the Lord. Therefore comfort one another with these words' " (1 Thess. 4:17–18).

❧   ❧   ❧

If you should be reading these lamentations of a modern father, who has struggled agonizingly with the departure of his son to heaven, and you're not sure where you will spend eternity, Wes isn't here to tell you, but temporarily I am. In fact, I can't think of any other good reason for me to remain here on earth than to tell you how you can enter into what the apostle Paul called "that blessed hope." He urges you to "lay hold of eternal life," and how do you do that? You pray the prayer to which Jesus attached the guarantee: If you pray from your heart, you'll be forever His. The prayer is, " 'God, be merciful to me a sinner,' and receive me here and now into Your everlasting kingdom through my acceptance of Jesus Christ as my Lord and Savior. I thank you, Lord Jesus Christ."

So how do you know that you're forever His? Because the apostle Paul asserted that the answer to the question, "Who will ascend into heaven?" is "that if you confess with your mouth the Lord Jesus and believe in your heart that God has raised Him from the dead, you will be saved. For with the heart one believes to righteousness, and with the mouth confession is made to salvation. . . . For . . . 'whoever calls upon the name of the LORD shall be saved' " (Rom. 10:6, 9, 10, 13).

If you sincerely prayed that prayer, and have claimed Christ's promise in His Word that you have thereby become His, or if there's any other way I could help you—or, indeed, if you could help me—I hope that, right now, you will sit down and write to me.

Dr. John Wesley White
Box 120
Markham, Ontario L3P 7R5
Canada